# PRAISE FOR *PRACTIC*

"Janet Ply is the real deal. I've seen way too many talented people flail in leadership because nobody ever taught them how to do the job well. This book fixes that. Janet has been in the fire, she's led through chaos, and now she's giving you the tools she's used to rescue high-stakes, high-dollar messes. If you lead people—or you want to—*Practical Leadership* should live on your desk. Get it, use it, lead better."

—**MEL ROBBINS,** *New York Times* bestselling author of *The Let Them Theory* and host of *The Mel Robbins Podcast*

"Janet Ply has created what so many leadership books promise but rarely deliver—a practical and actionable guide, grounded in real-world experience. With clarity and compassion, she cuts through the noise and gives leaders exactly what they need: a framework that works in the messiness of real organizations. Whether you're new to leadership or trying to rebuild your confidence after years in the trenches, this book will equip you to lead with greater trust, accountability, and purpose. It's not just theory—it's a road map for real transformation."

—**DR. MARSHALL GOLDSMITH,** Thinkers50 #1 executive coach and *New York Times* bestselling author of *The Earned Life, Triggers,* and *What Got You Here Won't Get You There*

"What a find! Janet Ply offers hard-won wisdom from her own successful career as a corporate turnaround expert in compelling page after page. Searingly honest and highly actionable, *Practical Leadership* is an invaluable resource for new and experienced leaders alike."

—**AMY C. EDMONDSON,** Novartis Professor of Leadership, Harvard Business School, and author of *Right Kind of Wrong*

"*Practical Leadership* bridges the gap between knowing and doing. Janet Ply's actionable tactics make leadership skills accessible and achievable."

—**DORIE CLARK,** *Wall Street Journal* bestselling author
of *The Long Game* and one of Thinkers50's
Top Business Thinkers in the World

"*Practical Leadership* is the book I wish I'd had at the start of my career, and it still has plenty I can use today. Few things are more important—and less understood—than what it takes to lead effectively. Janet Ply diagnoses the most common challenges with clarity and empathy and offers a deeply practical path forward. She closes by saying, 'Everyone deserves to work for a great leader.' With this guide in hand, that aspiration feels possible."

—**CHRIS HYAMS,** former CEO, Indeed

"At long last—a leadership book that gets to the heart of what really works and skips the fluff. This book is a gift to every high performer who was promoted into a leadership role without a map (which is nearly everyone). If you're jaded by generic advice and need actionable insights and practices you can use starting today, *Practical Leadership* is a fantastic resource."

—**JAMES M. CITRIN,** CEO, Spencer Stuart, and bestselling author
of *You're in Charge, Now What?* and *The Career Playbook*

"Janet Ply strips away the noise of leadership theory and delivers what today's leaders truly need—practical, real-world tactics. *Practical Leadership* is a blueprint for those who've been thrust into leadership without a road map. Janet's relatable stories and actionable framework will resonate with anyone who wants to lead with authenticity, confidence, and results."

—**ASHEESH ADVANI,** CEO, JA (Junior Achievement) Worldwide,
and coauthor of *Modern Achievement*

"Janet Ply has written a fluff-free guide for leaders. Real strategies, real moves, and real results—all before your coffee gets cold."

—**MIKE MICHALOWICZ,** author of *All In* and *Profit First*

"Real leadership begins with yourself. In *Practical Leadership*, Janet Ply reminds us that when leaders are aligned with themselves and authentically connect to others, they can build the trust needed to unlock the full potential of their teams."

—**HORTENSE LE GENTIL,** executive leadership coach, keynote speaker, and author of *The Unlocked Leader*

"What I appreciate most about *Practical Leadership* is its unapologetic clarity. Janet Ply doesn't romanticize leadership; she demystifies it, breaking it into specific, actionable behaviors anyone can learn. With warmth and wisdom, she shows that excellence and empathy are not mutually exclusive. This book is the guide I wish every new (and seasoned) leader had."

—**GENA COX, PHD,** organizational psychologist, Thinkers50 Top 50 global coach, and award-winning author of *Leading Inclusion*

"In a world saturated with leadership advice, Janet Ply cuts through the noise with rare clarity and grounded wisdom. This book doesn't offer gimmicks—it offers truth. With humility and conviction, Janet invites us to become the kind of leaders others trust with their full humanity. If you're ready to trade performative leadership for the kind that actually transforms people and systems, this is your guide."

—**RON CARUCCI,** cofounder and managing partner, Navalent; bestselling, award-winning author of *Rising to Power* and *To Be Honest*

"There are a million leadership books out there, but very few have the breadth—from communication to productivity to hiring and retention—and combination of real-world tools and instructive storytelling of *Practical Leadership*. This is a powerful handbook for leaders at any level."

—**PAUL EPSTEIN,** former NFL and NBA executive and bestselling author of *The Power of Playing Offense* and *Better Decisions Faster*

"The title says it all. If you are a high achiever grappling with the complexities of leadership, *Practical Leadership* is for you. Janet Ply gives you not only the 'why' behind various aspects of leadership but also the very practical 'how-to' for applying the insights to your own unique situation. Whether you are new to leading others or an old hand, there is a lot to learn from this gem of a book."

—**MARGARET ANDREWS,** Harvard instructor, managing director of the MYLO Center, and author of *Manage Yourself to Lead Others*

"Leadership is multifaceted, requiring great agility, empathy, and foresight. *Practical Leadership* provides the decoder ring for leadership success. By providing practical, tactical advice and guidance based on decades of experience, Janet Ply helps anyone stepping into a leadership role or those who are expanding theirs. Every leader needs this book on their desks and in their hands."

—**MATT ABRAHAMS,** lecturer, Stanford Graduate School of Business; author of *Think Faster, Talk Smarter: How to Speak Successfully When You're Put on the Spot*; and host of *Think Fast, Talk Smart: The Podcast*

"Leadership is a lifelong commitment to learning and growth. *Practical Leadership* delivers what most leadership books don't: clear, actionable tactics for real challenges. Leaders at all levels of experience will benefit from the examples and lessons found in this unique book."

—**MARK BOSTER, PHD,** former CIO, US Department of Justice

"*Practical Leadership* delivers what is often lacking in the development of leaders: a clear, actionable framework for leading people while delivering measurable results. Janet Ply brings a rare ability to translate theory into practical tools that can be immediately applied in complex, real-world environments. I had the privilege of working with Janet during our time at NFP and witnessed firsthand the profound impact her leadership training had on individuals and teams alike. Her approach consistently elevates leaders, helping them not only grow but also scale their influence across the organization."

—**MARK GROSVENOR,** EVP and CTO, NFP

"Leadership isn't about being perfect—it's about being present, making thoughtful decisions, and earning the trust of those you serve. *Practical Leadership* brings heart and honesty to the often messy reality of leading people, while never losing sight of the goal: delivering results that matter. With wisdom rooted in real experience, Janet Ply has created a guide that helps leaders show up with clarity, courage, and compassion—and drive the kind of performance that builds strong teams and lasting impact."

—**BARBARA SUGG,** former president and CEO,
Southwest Power Pool

# PRACTICAL
# LEADERSHIP

## A Guide to
## BUILDING TRUST,
## GETTING RESULTS,
## and CHANGING LIVES

# JANET PLY, PhD

PP

*Practical Leadership: A Guide to Building Trust,*
*Getting Results, and Changing Lives*

ISBN: 978-1-7368778-2-1 (paperback)
ISBN: 978-1-7368778-3-8 (ebook)

Library of Congress Control Number: 2025913465

Editing by Kristina Paider, Maren Showkeir, Carolyn Johnson, and Brandon Coward
Cover and interior design by Caitlin Smith
Author photo by Nids Creations Photography
Brain illustration by Jonathan Kaut

Published by Pendére Press, Lakewood Ranch, FL

*To all the high achievers who stepped into leadership roles
without a road map and were expected
to figure it out on their own.*

# CONTENTS

INTRODUCTION

# LET'S GET PRACTICAL

**I'VE SPENT THREE DECADES RUNNING COMPLEX,** high-visibility, and high-stress corporate programs across multiple industries, with budgets ranging in size from modest to hundreds of millions of dollars. In working both as an outside consultant and as a full-time employee in roles ranging from project manager to senior leader, the biggest lesson I've learned is that success almost always comes down to one word: leadership (or lack thereof).

This fact probably doesn't come as a surprise to anyone. But what shocked me early in my career—and often still does—is how unprepared many people are for taking on leadership roles. I'm equally astounded by how impractical most corporate thinking is when it comes to setting up leaders for success.

In my work as a consultant in particular, much of my time has been spent helping organizations recover large programs whose failure can frequently be attributed to a clear deficit of practical leadership skills.

The cost of leaders who struggle and fail—failure being defined as when a leader's actions or inactions result in negative consequences for their team or organization for a variety of reasons—is staggering.

Of the estimated seven million business leaders in the US, most are winging it—trying to figure it out as they go along. And it's not working very well. Statistics from the Center for Creative Leadership indicate that approximately 40 percent of new leaders fail within their first eighteen months.[1] The data isn't any better for executives. According to a report from Developmental Dimensions International Inc., HR considers about half of the executives hired externally to be failures in their role.[2] Internally promoted executives fail at a rate of slightly more than a third.

A 2024 *Harvard Business Review* article based on a Gartner analysis of more than 9,000 employees and managers found that nearly half of managers (48 percent) are at risk of failure and that employees reporting to those managers are 91 percent less likely to be high performers, three times more likely to want to leave their organizations, and four times more likely to underperform on both customer satisfaction and innovation goals.[3]

Leaders at all levels, including C-suite and senior executives, have shared their imposter syndrome with me and questioned their ability to lead. They admit that they don't have the difficult conversations that need to be had; they lack confidence in their interviewing and hiring skills; they don't feel they are very effective at setting goals and executing; and several have asked what to say in one-on-one meetings with their direct reports.

Some of the programs I've helped fix were set up to fail from the start. How can that be? If a leader makes a bad or misinformed decision, such as imposing an unrealistic completion date; doesn't provide enough of or the right people to do the work; or fails to understand the needed oversight, the outcomes are almost always unfavorable. I've witnessed program cost and schedule overruns that were double, triple, or even more. And I saw this on several engagements.

To be clear, these failures of leadership are most often not the fault of the individual, though they of course bear some responsibility and certainly are held accountable. Most leaders are promoted to leadership positions because they performed their tasks well in a previous role. The challenge comes when they are expected to automagically figure out what it means to be a leader and to realize, as Marshall Goldsmith famously said, "What got you here won't get you there."

Training at most companies—if it is ever provided—usually consists of generic online training programs that must be taken after hours and feature content that is of little value. And because your manager and your manager's manager were probably expected to figure out themselves how to lead, they aren't always the best mentors. They're still trying, though most probably wouldn't admit it, to learn how to lead as well.

Tens of thousands of books have been written on myriad topics associated with leadership—ownership, accountability, alignment, productivity, execution, strategic planning, communications, and so on. No new leader has time to read all of these books. And even if you did, they contain countless seemingly (or actually) mixed messages:

- "Be authentic" (Brené Brown, *Dare to Lead*)
- "Adapt your style"
  (Ken Blanchard, *The Situational Leader*)

- "Double down on your strengths"
  (Tom Rath, *StrengthsFinder 2.0*)
- "Work on your weaknesses"
  (Jim Collins, *Good to Great*)

- "Lead from the front"
  (Jocko Willink and Leif Babin, *Extreme Ownership*)
- "Delegate and empower"
  (Stephen R. Covey, *The 7 Habits of Highly Effective People*)

A further challenge is that every company has its own culture and values. Expectations differ from one manager to the next in the same company. Each person has a unique personality and beliefs. You can succeed under one manager and fail under the next one. New people are brought in and others leave. External factors such as acquisitions, competition, technological disruptions, and economic challenges create a need for leaders to adapt to changes on a regular basis.

As an engineer and a systems thinker by nature, this frustrated but also intrigued me. Creating a practical framework of processes and steps that would apply to most leadership situations and prospective leaders seemed difficult. But I was convinced that—just like any problem—it *could* be solved.

So, in 2019, I began developing the Practical Leadership Workshop and the accompanying Practical Leadership Framework, which focused on the most common things I observed leaders struggling with, addressed frequently asked questions, and combined the best advice of thousands of business books, TED Talks, podcasts, and research reports with twenty-five years of in-the-trenches experience to create the most practical, efficient, and effective system for taking leaders from here to there.

Since then, I've partnered with companies big and small—and the results have been phenomenal, with more than 75 percent of attendees having been promoted at least once and others having been promoted multiple times, including up to senior vice president. Executives have told me that my work has transformed their departments, creating higher productivity, higher employee engagement, and less turnover.

If you're a leader who feels unprepared, overwhelmed, or even afraid to ask for help—you're not alone! I've been where you are. The system outlined in this book has given me and hundreds of my clients a practical road map to overcoming those feelings and becoming the successful leader they know they're capable of being.

I'm confident it will work for you too.

# CHAPTER ONE

# MANAGEMENT IS NOT LEADERSHIP

**THE ALARM WENT OFF AT 5:00 A.M.,** like it did every morning. I got up, got dressed, and headed to the barn with my sisters to milk the cows before breakfast and school. My parents raised my two sisters and me on a small farm in Sulphur Springs, Arkansas (population: 243).

During the summers, we added working in our garden, bushhogging pastures, and cutting firewood to our usual list of chores. Both my parents were hard workers, probably to a fault, and instilled their work ethic in me. Dad would say repeatedly, "Get a good education and work hard, and you'll always have a job."

I vividly remember sitting in a lawn chair under the large pine trees in our yard, shucking ears of corn and thinking, *I don't know what I'm going to do when I grow up, but it's not going to be working in the hot sun, getting chiggers from picking blackberries, and cleaning out manure in a barn. If all I need to do is go to college and work hard, that's easier than what I'm doing now.*

Few people could outwork me. I finished my undergraduate degree in three years, taking a heavy course load while working to pay for college. My last year, I worked as a checker in a

Safeway grocery store, averaging twenty-five to thirty-five hours a week in addition to classes.

When I graduated from college, I was offered a position as a manager trainee at Safeway. Maybe Dad was right. My hard work and education were already paying off. I had a job opportunity that paid more than double what programmer jobs were paying, which was what I had planned to do upon graduation.

Over the years, I went back to college for three graduate degrees and continued to move into larger roles. My managers loved how much work I got done, my dependability, and my drive to learn and improve. I thought I was a natural leader; getting results came easily for me. No matter how hard I worked or how many hours I put in, it was easier than milking cows and picking, shelling, or shucking vegetables from the garden.

Like most people promoted into management roles, I took a personality assessment, in this case, the Myers-Briggs survey. This self-administered assessment is designed to help people understand their personality type, strengths, and preferences and to better understand how they relate to others who have different personality types.

My personality profile was ENTJ (extroverted, intuitive, thinking, judging), a profile with characteristics, according to the assessment, that make "natural" leaders. I took that to heart, which led me to the conclusion that my way of doing things must be right. Work hard and keep learning. I continued with my game plan, which seemed to be working well. Until it didn't.

Just because my profile was described as a natural leader didn't resolve the flaws that would cause me to flounder, and even fail, in leadership roles. I began to learn that my work ethic superpower didn't always translate into good leadership skills.

I was still getting up at five o'clock and was at work by six thirty or seven; I would leave each evening at seven or later. I worked most weekends. My to-do list kept me focused, and my reputation for getting things done fed my ego.

And then it all changed. The leaders where I worked participated in a 360-degree feedback review. A survey was sent to each leader's direct reports, peers, managers, and others we worked with, asking for feedback on our performance. Yes, the results of my survey gave me kudos for hard work, but other comments hit me like a ton of bricks. Some of the feedback said that people saw me as intimidating and rigid and as someone who moved too quickly. During interactions, I could be insensitive to people's feelings. Not everyone wanted to work with me. One commented that it was "my way or the highway."

When I met with the company representative who administered the survey to review my results, I sat in the meeting with my arms folded and said, "I run the project management office. I'm on the hook for the successful delivery of more than seventy-five projects totaling tens of millions of dollars. It's my responsibility to set the guidelines for how we manage projects. It's natural for people to view me as being rigid. They don't want to follow the processes we have in place and change how they work. I have high expectations, and not everyone wants to put in the work to meet them. I get why people may not want to work for me. I want to work with people who want to get things done."

I went home at the end of a twelve-hour day and sulked. I felt like all my hard work and achievements didn't mean much. I couldn't stop thinking about the comments. *Janet's too rigid. Janet wants things done her way and isn't open to the opinions of others. Janet can be intimidating and shuts people down when she meets with them if they disagree with her.* I started wondering if maybe I wasn't cut out to be a leader.

The next day, I met with my manager, Mike, who was also a good mentor. He had read the survey results and knew I'd be upset. "Janet, you are a valued member of the leadership team. You get more done in a day than most people do in a week. That is an important part of being a leader, and you've mastered that. Leadership is also about people. View the 360 feedback as an opportunity for learning about the human side. You'll be unstoppable."

## THE IMPORTANCE OF TRUST

That night, I went home and reflected on the 360 comments and my conversation with Mike.

It honestly hadn't occurred to me—and I'd never received any training to warn or guide me—that my workaholic schedule was causing stress for others by setting a bar so high that they were missing personal and family time or working while on vacation. My philosophy was that we were being paid to get results. Anything that stood in the way of that was almost always just an excuse. And it wasn't like we were picking blackberries for fourteen hours.

This mindset created a massive lack of trust within my team—to which I was completely blind and, candidly, uncaring. They felt like when the rubber met the road, they couldn't trust me to act in their interests in a variety of areas: from allowing them time off when they needed to be with their families to not being receptive to their ideas to not taking into account their career goals and individual needs.

Then things changed in my own life that made me realize that more important things exist outside of work. I became a co-parent to two young children, ages one and two. The transition from the single lifestyle to parenting turned my world upside down. Until then, I had no idea of the sacrifices parents make to find day care; to get their kids to doctor appointments; or to attend their school, church, and sports events. I hadn't given much thought to how they stay up all night with a sick child and somehow muster the energy to go to work the next day and still do their job. Becoming a parent overnight felt overwhelming. I remember calling my younger sister with this advice: "If you're going to have kids, do it now while you're young. You'll need all the energy you can get!"

During this same time, my mom started having health issues. Dad took her to numerous doctors for a diagnosis, yet her health continued to decline with no medical answers. I'd travel from Virginia to Arkansas when I could. One night after work, my older sister called to tell me that Mom had been diagnosed with ALS (amyotrophic lateral sclerosis, also known as Lou Gehrig's disease). I was one thousand miles away from her and felt the constant pull on my heartstrings because I couldn't be there for her as much as I wanted to be. I saw the sacrifices of my two sisters, making long drives to be with her on weekends and using vacation and holiday time to spend with her. They had to balance work and kids and their own lives. They were exhausted most of the time, and I was too far away to be of much help.

During the first visit back home after her diagnosis, I could tell she was moving slower and resting more. The next time I visited, she had started using a wheelchair. She always liked having a pretty yard and used a grabber to pick up pine cones and limbs as she wheeled around the lawn. The next visit after that, she was using an oxygen machine. Then a hospital bed replaced her normal bed. Every visit seemed to be a gut punch.

It was during this time of dealing with a new family and my mom's terminal illness that I realized that I wasn't the only person navigating life's challenges. Several people at work shared that they, too, were dealing with aging parents, issues with kids, or their own personal struggles. In spite of this, many of my coworkers and team members took on extra burdens to cover for me when I needed it most. I didn't have to ask any of them. Once they knew my situation, they stepped up. Because it was the right thing to do.

Combined with Mike's advice and the feedback from the 360, I'd reached a critical turning point in how I viewed my role at work. I realized that the work-hard-and-learn game plan for success that Dad had given me had turned me into an excellent manager—capable of creating and executing (on my part) processes, systems, and plans that got the best results—and fast-tracked my career. But it also produced a toxic environment with my colleagues that was ultimately unsustainable.

To be a true leader, I needed to apply the same systems-based tactics to learning how to lead people as I did for projects: take a problem, break it down into its smallest components, research the root cause(s) of the problem, develop solutions, test them, and tweak as needed.

## LEADERSHIP IS EASIER THAN YOU THINK—IT'S TACTICAL

The people side didn't come easily for me. Humans are messy.

Everyone has different perspectives, opinions, and ideas. Some work harder than others. Some are introverts, and others are extroverts.

But what I eventually discovered was that leadership isn't that complicated. You don't have to be a natural-born leader or have a certain personality or even be the best and brightest.

You don't need five hundred hours of leadership training or to work sixty hours a week or to visit a coach or therapist to make you a better leader. It doesn't need to cause the physical toll and emotional pain associated with anxiety, overwhelm, frustration, and self-doubt.

Leadership isn't an art or a mystery to be solved. It's tactical and can be learned.

Why do I believe this? Because it's worked for me in my career and for hundreds of leaders I've coached and who have attended my workshops.

Let's look at a few examples.

## TACTICS IN REAL LIFE

Michael had a great reputation for performing well as an analyst in the technology department of a health-care company. Like so many others, because of his successes in earlier positions, he had been promoted to a leadership role. And like most leaders, he was provided minimal training and little clarity about expectations in his new position.

"Honestly, I'm frustrated and overwhelmed right now," Michael told me during one of our early coaching sessions. "I feel pressured to figure things out, but I don't know what I'm supposed to be doing. I need to learn to delegate but feel like I need to do it myself if I want it done right."

He continued, "Everything has become so reactive, and

I can't get ahead. It seems like no one is following the rules and everything turns into an escalation and an exception. I'm unsure where to start, and I don't want to say the wrong thing. Allison wants to improve the team culture and is asking people what they enjoy doing to make them happier. How far do I have to go to accommodate people's desires? Do I have to make everyone on my team happy? I'm feeling a little lost."

His previous manager had been replaced by Allison, who also had come up through the ranks as a high performer and had been promoted into a senior leadership role.

He acknowledged that he often talked too much in meetings and didn't get the results needed for knowing what work to get done. "When I'm in meetings with Allison, she seems to know what questions to ask and the right work to prioritize. How do I learn this? How do I figure out how to prioritize and assign work?" Michael asked me. "Allison just seems like a natural-born leader."

That's when I told Michael, "Allison once felt the same way as you do. She also wondered if she wasn't cut out for her leadership role."

I knew this because, a year earlier, I had been Allison's coach. She had talked about her challenges: an overwhelming workload, feeling out of control leading a technical team, unable to get ahead, and unsure of how to communicate with executives.

Michael and I started with the basics relevant to his situation. We worked on setting goals and priorities so he knew the most important work to focus on and how to set clear expectations for his team. Then he learned how to delegate properly and stopped doing the work himself. He took a systematic approach and built on the tactics over time. He was able to get control of his time, build trust with his team and managers, and get more done by implementing the tactics associated with each of these areas. And you can too.

When I first started working with Allison, Michael's manager, she believed that she had to know everything that her team members knew. She had moved up quickly in the company, starting as an analyst and then as a project manager. She had recently been promoted to director. The scope of her new role included overseeing teams of highly technical people (software architects, developers, and engineers), many of whom she had not worked with directly.

A self-described severe type-A perfectionist, Allison felt determined to gain what she saw as necessary technical expertise. She had started taking online courses in various technical areas. The learning curve that accompanied the new scope of work, meeting team members, figuring out team relationship dynamics, and trying to gain technical knowledge was intensive and left her drained at the end of each day.

In our coaching session, Allison said, "How can I possibly manage, inspire, and gain the respect of developers, architects, and engineers when I have zero technical knowledge? Unless I know what my team knows, they won't view me as a leader. If I start asking questions, they'll wonder why I'm in my role instead of one of them. Maybe I wonder that as well."

Allison had an internal fear of failing as a leader. She had built her career on being able to figure things out and get the job done. But this role felt different. She worried that asking for help would be a signal to her manager and her peers that she was unqualified. At home, she was the primary breadwinner, so losing her job or getting a demotion would be devastating, which added to her already high stress level.

We used tactics to shift Allison's belief from a perceived

need to learn technical skills to one of integrating her business skills with her team members' strengths and experience. She took an inventory of her skills and her employees' skills and compared them to the work her department delivered. This new perspective allowed her to highlight team member expertise and contributions while bringing her business acumen to the table. Her team appreciated her bigger-picture insights and understood the importance of their work to the company.

This one tactic of employing a skills inventory gave Allison permission to stop using her time to learn technical things, which freed up time to work on the most important things and get back to a healthy work-life balance.

"What do you wish you had known earlier?" I asked Allison later.

Without missing a beat, she replied, "Not being the expert in the room is the best advantage to have."

Michael's story, Allison's story, and maybe *your* story are relatable because they're so common.

Simple tools and tactics to improve leadership skills don't mean it's easy. Developing into a great leader is hard work and a lifelong journey. It's about changing or replacing bad habits and limiting beliefs that have been ingrained in us for decades.

It takes a lot of self-discipline and intentionality to continue improving, and enhancing leadership skills is no different. Many tactics are easy to implement and seem like more of a tweak or an epiphany of "Why didn't I think of that?" Sometimes we just need to be reminded: include an agenda in all your meeting invitations.

Some tactics are simply tools you can use to help in specific areas, while others require more effort and self-discipline.

The good news is that you don't need to do everything

at once. Sometimes one seemingly small adjustment is a game changer.

To help organize tactics, I developed the Practical Leadership Framework to guide you through the most important and common aspects of leadership, both the task focus and the people side.

Let's look at the six components of the framework and what is included in each one.

## PRACTICAL LEADERSHIP FRAMEWORK OVERVIEW

Like most undertakings, foundational understandings and skills are developed and built on. A basketball player learns how to dribble, pass, shoot a basketball, and understand the rules before playing a real game. A student doesn't learn mathematics by learning calculus. They master addition, subtraction, multiplication, and division before moving on to algebra, geometry, and trigonometry. Then the student is ready to tackle calculus.

The same is true of a leadership journey. If leaders knew what to do, no doubt they would do it. Too often, however, they haven't been properly trained in the fundamentals, don't know what questions to ask, and/or haven't had great mentors.

The Practical Leadership Framework reveals and provides tactics for mastering the components on which leadership is built. These six elements are not isolated—they are interconnected. While some naturally build upon others, all must work together as a cohesive system for a leader to reach their full potential.

A leader who consistently leads by example and earns trust is more likely to develop strong self-awareness, communicate effectively, build high-performing teams, and drive meaningful results. On the other hand, a gap in any one of the six areas will likely undermine the others, limiting overall leadership effectiveness.

This book is organized into six sections that correspond to each area in the framework. As you read each section, consider how the concepts relate to and influence the other dimensions of leadership. Strengthening one area will often strengthen others.

The Practical Leadership Framework equips you with the tactics, tools, and resources you need to become a trusted leader who delivers results and influences lives. It addresses the behaviors that leaders strive to model and provides guidance on how to get results.

At the heart of the framework is **Lead by Example**, where you'll learn how to model the behavior you want to see, build trust with your team, create a safe and supportive work environment, and understand the mindset shifts you'll need to make as your leadership responsibility increases.

You'll develop **Awareness** by applying tactics to master emotional intelligence, recognizing and overcoming biases, and leveraging diverse perspectives for collaboration and innovation.

The tactics in the framework teach you **Effective Communication,** including how to have difficult conversations, set clear expectations, and become an active listener.

Additionally, you'll be given practical strategies to optimize your **Productivity Habits,** such as minimizing distractions, delegating effectively, and running productive meetings.

The **Exceptional Results** section provides a goal-setting process that helps you prioritize and plan work to deliver the highest-value outcomes.

The final section reveals tactics for building and maintaining **High-Performing Teams** by hiring top talent, retaining your best people, and addressing performance challenges.

The majority of a leader's role falls into one of these six categories, all of which are interrelated and all of which can be learned by understanding the concepts and implementing the tactics provided.

## CHANGING LIVES—BIRD BY BIRD

At this point, you might be feeling overwhelmed by the Practical Leadership Framework and all the things you need to learn. The good news is that you don't have to implement everything all at once. Sometimes just a few small tweaks or changes can lead to huge results.

The title of author Anne Lamott's book *Bird by Bird* is based on a story she tells about her dad. Her brother was given a school project on birds and was overwhelmed by the assignment. Her father told him to take his project bird by bird. Lamott teaches her student writers to go bird by bird—or in other words, focus on small steps instead of the entire project. The same applies to building your leadership skills. Implement one or two tactics first.

I've worked with hundreds of people and have seen them get promoted multiple times, deliver outstanding results in a normal workday, develop team skills and relationships, and spend time with family and friends.

For me, I still get up early to start my routine. Then I usually write or develop course materials. Sometimes, when the words aren't coming or when I'm frustrated because I've written one section ten different times, I remember that it's still easier than milking cows or picking blackberries in the hot sun. It's about putting in the reps, bird by bird, and being better today than yesterday.

I'm not the same leader today as I was when I first started managing people. I've learned how to apply frameworks, processes, assessments, and other tools to become better. Instead of the earlier comments I got on 360 reviews, I now receive feedback like this from the president of a client company: *Janet is a tireless worker who leads by example and believes in enabling a team by teaching and coaching, not by commanding. This instills confidence and leaves behind inspired professionals, prepared to succeed again and again.*

As a successful leader, you don't just change your life for the better. You make a difference in the lives of many people, extending beyond team members and colleagues to their families and friends. You create a culture where people want to work and help one another. You may be the reason why a team member's marriage works or the joy they feel when attending family events. Leadership is not just about what you get done; it's about the people whose lives you change.

Now let's get started.

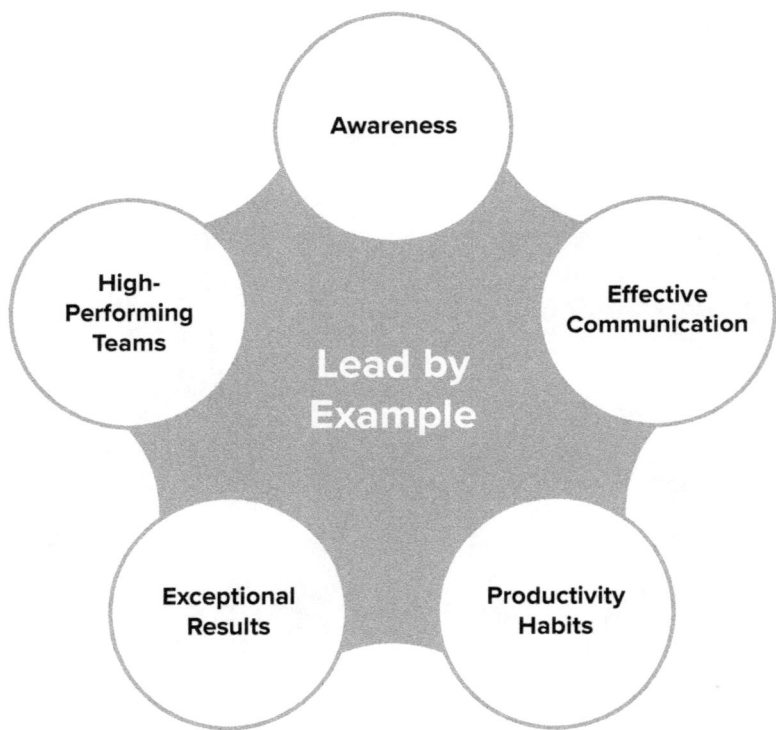

Awareness

Effective Communication

Productivity Habits

Exceptional Results

High-Performing Teams

Lead by Example

# PART ONE

---

# LEAD BY EXAMPLE

Good actions give strength to ourselves
and inspire good actions in others.

**—PLATO**

**LEADERSHIP ISN'T ABOUT TELLING PEOPLE WHAT TO DO**—it's
about modeling the behaviors you want them to have. As social
creatures, we are wired to observe and mimic those in positions
of authority, instinctively following the leader's cues to fit in
and be accepted. This tribal instinct is embedded in workplace
dynamics. Every action a leader takes—whether intentional or
not—sets the tone for the organization or their team.

# CHAPTER TWO
# PEOPLE MIMIC THE LEADER

**GREG, THE PRESIDENT OF A COMPANY** I was working for, asked me to present the findings of my operations department assessment to his executive team at their weekly meeting. I was first on the agenda and joined the video meeting a few minutes before it started. Others, including Greg, joined a couple of minutes late, and several people began talking about what they did over the weekend. Greg eventually pulled up the agenda and shared his screen—fifteen minutes later.

Once I started my presentation, participants had a semblance of engagement, but I could see that several were shifting their attention between the meeting screen and another monitor. When I finished, a couple of people asked questions, most of which I had already covered. It was a frustrating meeting for me but seemed like status quo for them.

Not too long after the unfocused meeting with Greg's team, the CIO of a manufacturing company, Carolyn, asked me to present my assessment findings I had done for her to her leadership team. What a difference in this meeting! She sent out a complete agenda two days in advance along with the assessment, asking people to review ahead of time. The meeting started and ended on time. Everyone was engaged and focused. They asked questions during the presentation and made decisions on the priority and plan for implementing the recommendations. Everyone left the meeting with their marching orders.

How does it happen that two executive-level meetings can be so different? It starts with our natural instinct to follow the leader.

## WE ARE A TRIBAL SPECIES

Humans have a natural inclination to belong to a group. For two hundred thousand years, being a tribe member delivered a significant survival advantage. A person wouldn't last long against the dangers in the wilderness and the environmental challenges and hazards. Being part of a strong tribe increased the survival odds substantially. (Tribe 14, Saber-Tooth Tigers 3.)

Belonging also came with responsibilities and assumptions that your behavior would align with tribal norms, especially the leader who set expectations. A person who didn't follow the rules would be left behind, so complying with the leader was important for survival. This is still true today but in different ways.

The concept of tribal belonging extends beyond affiliation; it encompasses a set of norms, values, and expectations that govern behavior within the group. It's why we sign up for activities, attend a particular church, or support our favorite teams.

Our tribal tendencies are in part explained by mirror neurons. These specialized brain cells activate when a person performs an action and when they observe someone else performing the same action. They help us understand the emotions and intentions of others. For example, if you smile or wave at someone, they usually smile or wave back. Your brain's mirror neurons fire in a way that simulates the feeling of smiling or waving. Both people empathized with the emotional state. Have you ever laughed so hard that you couldn't stop and the people around you started laughing as well? When you smile, your team members smile back. This simple act increases feelings of positivity.

Mirror neurons also contribute to imitation, which is an important part of social learning. We learn by observing and copying the actions and behaviors of those around us, particularly those within our tribe or social group. This helps reinforce cultural norms, shared behaviors, and cooperation within the group.

When I worked in the Washington, DC, area, most senior leaders dressed in formal business attire, and the employees in those companies dressed similarly. While working for a software company in Texas, its founder and CEO wore T-shirts, shorts, and tennis shoes. Within a day or two, the new hires were wearing the same casual attire.

Almost every aspect of leaders' behavior is observed: what time they get to work, how late they stay, how they dress, how they handle situations, how they treat people.

The roles of mirror neurons and cultural norms highlight why it's so important for you to lead by example. You define the attitudes, behaviors, and emotional state of your team and determine the culture and work environment. It all starts with you.

## ASSESSING LEADERSHIP BEHAVIORS

Lead by Example is at the center of the Practical Leadership Framework for a reason—it's foundational to the other five areas. You won't be successful if you aren't leading your team by modeling the behaviors you want to see in them.

We've all experienced people in leadership roles whom we admire as well as those we want to avoid. Where do you fall?

The chart that follows is an assessment that includes important behaviors to consider in your leadership role. Reflect on each question and be honest with yourself. Write the numbers from the following rating scale in the last column and add them up at the end:

- 1 = I nailed it
- 2 = Most of the time
- 3 = Probably need to improve

| BEHAVIOR | DESCRIPTION | RATING |
|---|---|---|
| Integrity | Consistently acts with honesty and ethical principles, aligns words and actions, does what's right, even when no one is watching. | |
| Positive Attitude | Maintains a positive outlook, even during challenging times; inspires others to stay motivated and engaged; encourages the team to focus on solutions over problems; looks for the good in situations and people. | |

| | | |
|---|---|---|
| **Accountability** | Owns outcomes, both successes and failures; holds oneself responsible for results; sets clear goals and is accountable for self and team performance; admits when a mistake was made without making excuses or blaming others. | |
| **Communication** | Actively listens, pays attention during meetings, sets clear expectations for team members, communicates clearly, provides regular feedback, receives constructive feedback without being defensive, articulates roles and responsibilities, provides clear direction during change. | |
| **Collaboration** | Encourages teamwork, inclusiveness, open communication, and cooperation; asks everyone for their ideas and perspectives in decision-making meetings, not just the people who voluntarily speak up. | |

| | | |
|---|---|---|
| **Emotional Intelligence** | Recognizes and manages emotions effectively, shows empathy and understands others' feelings, remains calm under pressure, helps a stressed team member through challenges, provides praise in public and constructive feedback in private, adjusts communication style based on individuals' personalities. | |
| **Work Ethic** | Demonstrates dedication, focus, and commitment to high performance; hires the best people for the job to build high-performing teams; shows up on time and prepared for meetings; ensures that meetings have an agenda or purpose with defined outcomes. | |
| **Consistency** | Proves reliable in actions and decisions, maintains a steady leadership behavior, consistently meets deadlines, responds to issues in a fair and predictable manner. | |

| | | |
|---|---|---|
| Empathy | Shows care and concern for others' well-being and actively listens to their concerns; proactively checks in on a team member who is struggling with a personal issue, offering support and flexibility. | |
| Adaptability | Demonstrates flexibility and openness to change, helps the team adjust to new circumstances, adapts to project scope or organizational changes, reassures the team, makes adjustments. | |
| Continuous Learning | Demonstrates a commitment to personal and professional growth and encourages others to grow, regularly attends training and shares insights with team members, provides development opportunities such as lunch-and-learns. | |

| Resilience | Bounces back from challenges and maintains a positive attitude during adversity, remains composed when faced with a failure, encourages the team to learn from mistakes and move forward. | |
|---|---|---|

How did you do? Would your team, manager, and peers score you differently? It's fine if you don't have a perfect score. It's why you're reading this book—you want to improve.

No one is perfect all the time and in all areas of leadership. Carolyn, the CIO described earlier as running effective meetings, also had a reputation for being fair, demonstrating empathy, communicating transparently to her teams, and remaining calm in high-stress meetings. Carolyn's 360-degree feedback review (more on these reviews later) had these positive comments:

- "Carolyn is the calmest and most rational person, even under stressful circumstances."
- "Carolyn always seeks out and listens to her team to understand their ideas."
- "Carolyn is the leader you want in the room when everything goes sideways."

She sounds like an ideal leader. However, the review also revealed that she struggled to act on a tenured leader who had toxic relationships with team members, with several leaving the company over a period of a few years as a result.

Carolyn's 360 feedback also included these comments:

- "Carolyn is loved by everyone, but employees wonder why she doesn't address the bad behavior of a leader on her team."
- "Carolyn does not address poor-performing employees as quickly as she should. This causes a lot of frustration and the perception that employees can get away with whatever they want."
- "Carolyn needs to hold team members accountable for their poor behavior."

Carolyn was loved by her team but had an issue that affected her credibility, caused frustration, and set an example that people didn't need to be accountable.

When she heard this feedback, she was disheartened for a minute but acknowledged it as legitimate. Having it in black and white in the 360 review comments (kindly worded) from her team helped. We had several coaching sessions, and she upleveled her skills in having difficult conversations and in addressing underperforming behavior. I'm happy to report that between the 360 review and the coaching, she took the appropriate action with the toxic leader.

No one is a perfect leader in all situations. That's OK. You can use feedback tools like the 360 review to find where you need to course-correct.

## ACTIONS SPEAK LOUDER THAN WORDS

Leadership is not about *telling* people what to do; rather, it's about *showing* them. One of the most important lessons in leadership is that actions speak louder than words. It's not just about what you say but about what you do. Your team watches everything you do and naturally mirrors your actions, attitudes, work ethic—almost everything.

When you say one thing but do another, you send mixed messages and quickly lose credibility. If Greg, who is always apologetically late to his meetings, told his leadership team that respecting people's time was important to him, they'd probably roll their eyes. If you tell employees that you want them to have a work-life balance and then email them at night and over the weekend, you're sending a mixed message. Do you tell your team that their feedback is valued and then become defensive or dismissive or make excuses when they give you constructive comments? Do you promote collaborative problem-solving but then give to the team the solution you want implemented? Do you promote flexibility and autonomy but then question every detail?

It's not uncommon for leaders to believe they're providing clear messaging when, in fact, they send mixed signals between their words and their actions. Consistency establishes you as trustworthy and reliable.

How you approach problems, handle stress, treat others, and participate in meetings are all unspoken standards for how your team should behave.

How do you treat people who clean the office? Are you respectful? Do you talk with them? Ignore them? During business-related meals with colleagues, do you show respect to your server? Are you empathetic when a parent leaves early to pick up a sick child from day care, or do you complain to others about having to do more work? Do you do what you say you'll do by the date you said you'd do it? Or do you offer excuses when something doesn't get done or change the deadline? Do you actively listen when someone brings you bad news and collaborate on how to mitigate the situation, or do you penalize the messenger? Does your team trust you to have their back?

Modeling the behaviors you want to see has more influence on your team than what you say. In which behavioral areas do you excel? Where could you improve? Strive to be better today than you were yesterday.

## MODELING WORK-LIFE BALANCE BEHAVIOR

One morning when I got to work, I found a sticky note on my monitor: "No one on their death bed ever wishes they had spent more time at work."

That note hit me like a ton of bricks, especially as it was not long after my mom had passed away. I reread the note. It was a reminder to me that I wished I had taken off work more and spent quality time with her. I can never get that time back, and it's one of my biggest regrets in life. I never found out who stuck the note to my monitor, but I'm glad they did. It's still a reminder to me when I think about what's important in life.

Leaders who believe that it's necessary to sacrifice their health, family, and personal growth for long hours at work to achieve career advancement are cooking up a recipe for burnout, resentment, and regret while putting mental and physical health at risk. Not to mention the bad example that is set for your team.

As a leader, you can safeguard your team by helping them balance professional responsibilities and personal well-being. Work-life balance for one person is not a one-size-fits-all concept. A person who has small children has different demands than someone who doesn't have kids. Some people prefer working in the office, while others prefer remote work or a hybrid. Someone may have an elderly parent to care for. If you're not sure what people need, you can always ask in your one-on-one meetings, which are covered in detail in chapter 3.

Establish your own work-life balance to lead by example. When you routinely drop your kids off at school before work or leave early to attend family events, you show it's acceptable to prioritize family time. If you send text messages or emails outside normal business hours, employees may feel pressured to reply.

Everyone understands that sometimes projects and assignments require more than a normal workweek. However, it's not sustainable to expect people to work extended hours. Overworked or stressed individuals are prone to burnout, which leads to declines in productivity and creativity. People need time to recharge and recover. A study conducted by Boston Consulting Group found that requiring overworked employees to take days, nights, or extended time off increased job satisfaction, open communication, and value delivery after only five months.[1] If you and your team are in a situation that requires extended long hours, be sure to schedule recovery time afterward.

Model the behavior you want to see from your team. When you show that work-life balance is a priority for yourself, it sends a powerful message that you not only value team members' professional contributions but also their well-being.

The way you lead your team could likely be the difference between whether a parent attends family events or is frustrated by missing out yet again because of a poorly planned deadline. It could be the difference between burnout and engagement. Leadership expert Simon Sinek says it perfectly: "Leadership is not about being in charge. Leadership is about taking care of those in your charge."[2]

As a leader, you genuinely care about your team and their well-being. You help them succeed. You're there for them when they need you to be. Sure, part of your job is setting the direction and getting things done. It's a lot easier when you have individuals who respect you and who are willing to do whatever it takes to help the team and the organization be successful.

People mimic the leader. Make sure your actions are worth mimicking and have a positive impact on those who are under your care.

CHAPTER THREE

# THE IMPORTANCE OF BELONGING

**HAVE YOU EVER BEEN IN A SITUATION** where you felt like you didn't belong? Maybe you weren't invited to a meeting or a team lunch. Or others on the team were sharing inside jokes and laughing at stories over the weekend. No one invited you into the conversation or offered to explain the jokes or asked about your weekend. The louder voices in the meeting dominated the conversation, and no one asked for your perspective. I think we can all relate to those types of feelings at some point during our personal or professional lives, thinking, *Maybe I just don't belong here.*

This is problematic for several reasons. When someone believes they don't belong in a company, they don't feel valued and start to become disengaged. Performance drops. You may lose opportunities to hear their ideas and perspectives. Over time, they will likely leave.

When a person wants to fit in, they may say or do things that don't reflect who they really are. This is a phenomenon known as masking, where an individual tries to conform to the environment by hiding their true feelings. This is more common than you may think.

A study by Deloitte found that 60 percent of people

downplay a part of themselves at work.[3] These percentages increase for people of color (69 percent) or those who are gay (65 percent). Pretending to be someone you are not is exhausting.

As a leader, it's important to embrace team members for who they are—their entire authentic self. You won't share the same beliefs in all areas or agree on everything. But it's in your best interest to create a culture of belonging so that people can be comfortable and feel accepted in their work life—not just because it's the right thing to do but also because it's a big factor for team success.

Employees who feel like they belong to an organization or a team are more engaged. Unfortunately, most organizations aren't doing a very good job of creating a culture of belonging. In the *Harvard Business Review* article "The Value of Belonging at Work," a group of behavioral experts at coaching consultancy BetterUp writes, "Social belonging is a fundamental human need, hardwired into our DNA. And yet, 40 percent of people say that they feel isolated at work, and the result has been lower organizational commitment and engagement. In a nutshell, companies are blowing it." They point out that employees who felt a sense of belonging had a 56 percent increase in job performance, a 50 percent drop in turnover risk, and a 75 percent reduction in sick days.[4]

How do you create a sense of belonging on your team? Let's look at ways to help with this.

## CREATE PSYCHOLOGICAL SAFETY TO BUILD TRUST

Early in my career, my philosophy was that my superiors trusted me. They knew I'd find a way to deliver and weren't interested in how I did it as long as people weren't quitting and HR wasn't getting complaints.

My ego liked that they viewed me as a go-to person for results. But, as mentioned earlier, my 360 review revealed flaws that suggested my team didn't trust me to have their backs or to take their personal lives into consideration if a deadline was looming. Most people who worked for me didn't feel comfortable asking if they could leave early to attend a school or family function, fearing I would view them unfavorably.

Amy Edmondson, professor of leadership and management at Harvard Business School and author of *The Fearless Organization: Creating Psychological Safety in the Workplace for Learning, Innovation, and Growth*, describes psychological safety as an environment of low interpersonal fear. People feel confident that they won't be punished or humiliated for voicing their opinions, discussing their ideas, or bringing concerns or mistakes to the table.[5] For example, you tell your direct reports that you will hold monthly one-on-one meetings with each of them and then cancel them because of work demands. In a psychologically safe environment, your direct reports would feel comfortable pointing out that you aren't holding up your end of the commitment. And you would thank them for bringing this to your attention and make the one-on-ones a high priority.

Google's Aristotle project underscores the importance of psychological safety. In 2012, Abeer Dubey, a manager on Google's People Analytics Team, led a research project that identified a successful team's key drivers. After years of analyzing data and interviews from more than 180 teams across the company, psychological safety emerged as the most important factor for team success.[6]

A common example I've seen is that leaders often promote work-life balance but reward overwork. They say, "We
value work-life balance, and we want you to take care of your
well-being." But when it comes to promotions, recognition, or
praise, they consistently reward those who stay late, respond
to emails on weekends, or go above and beyond at the cost
of their personal time. This double standard sends a message
that working long hours is the real path to success, undermining trust and discouraging employees from prioritizing their
well-being.

How comfortable would your team be to call you out if
you sent emails over the weekend after you've told everyone
they shouldn't be checking messages during nonwork hours?
Would they point out that you're saying one thing but doing
another? And how would you respond?

Have you ever said or heard someone else say, "I'm not
going to be the one to tell the boss bad news"? Think about
the issues created when people are afraid to bring concerns
to their manager. Problems that are not addressed up front,
when they can be mitigated more quickly, delay projects and
frustrate employees. The surprise factor causes many to look
bad to their managers and others.

People must be encouraged to speak up and know they
won't be blamed or reprimanded. You want to create an atmosphere where people are comfortable pushing back, sharing
ideas, communicating bad news, and taking calculated risks.
This kind of safe space is fundamental to a team's well-being,
open communication, and productivity.

One way to think about how to create this space is through
the lens of the psychological safety matrix, which Edmondson
developed to help people understand the relationship between

psychological safety and performance standards.[7] Consider a two-by-two matrix with Psychological Safety on the y-axis and Performance Standards on the x-axis. Each axis ranges from low to high. Let's look at each quadrant.

**Apathy Zone.** In the apathy zone, performance standards and psychological safety are low. Team members don't feel safe, nor are they engaged enough to care about their work. They want to fly under the radar, put forth minimal effort, show little interest in personal or team success, and avoid responsibility. They focus on protecting themselves versus doing work and are a drain on the team.

**Comfort Zone.** Our brains are wired to minimize change, so the comfort zone is, well, comfortable. Most people get along, but they aren't challenged. Team members feel safe and comfortable in their work environment. They aren't afraid of speaking up or making mistakes but lack the drive or pressure to perform at a high level. Companies with cultures of mediocrity tend to have a lot of employees clustered in the comfort zone quadrant. Performance standards are low, but people know they probably aren't going to get fired. I always say that there's no growth in the comfort zone.

**Anxiety Zone.** Performance standards and accountability are high in the anxiety zone, but psychological safety is low. Employees are held to high standards and are pressured to perform, but they don't feel safe or supported enough to offer new ideas, try new things, or make mistakes. They hesitate to bring bad news to the boss for fear of being berated or chastised. Trust is low, and employees focus on getting work done with minimal suggestions for improvement or innovation. They operate under stress and fear, which can lead to burnout, limited creativity, and disengagement. This is the environment that I likely created early in my career when all I focused on was getting things done without thinking about the people side.

**Learning Zone.** The learning zone is characterized by high performance standards and high psychological safety. This zone is the ideal environment for growth, creativity, and continuous improvement. Team members feel safe taking risks and are motivated to perform at their best. They are encouraged to collaborate, share ideas, make mistakes, and take risks without fear of judgment or reprimand. They provide constructive feedback. You want your team to operate in this quadrant.

It's important to know in which of the four zones you and your team operate so that you can course-correct as needed. The chart that follows offers a short assessment that you can use to better understand how your team members view psychological safety in the work environment.

Ask your team to anonymously score each statement, using the following ratings, and calculate the average:

- 1 = Strongly Disagree
- 2 = Disagree
- 3 = Neutral
- 4 = Agree
- 5 = Strongly Agree

Compare your results to theirs and see if they are aligned.

| PSYCHOLOGICAL SAFETY | |
| --- | --- |
| **Statement** | **Rating** |
| 1. I feel comfortable speaking up in meetings, even if my opinion and ideas differ from others. | |
| 2. If I make a mistake at work, I believe my team will treat it as a learning opportunity. | |
| 3. I feel respected by my teammates and leader, even when we have different perspectives. | |
| 4. I can ask other team members for help without worrying about being judged or seen as incompetent. | |
| 5. I feel safe taking risks and trying new things within my team. | |
| 6. I can openly discuss challenges or concerns with my team or leader without fear of blame or negative consequences. | |
| 7. Team members are accepted for who they are, even if they have different backgrounds or viewpoints. | |

| | |
|---|---|
| 8. When I speak up, I feel that my opinions are heard and valued by my teammates and leader. | |
| 9. The feedback I receive from other team members and my leader is constructive and focused on improvement rather than personal criticism. | |
| 10. I feel included and valued as a member of my team. | |
| **Total Psychological Safety Score** | |

Calculate the score by adding up the responses for each person on your team who completes the assessment and then taking the average. The minimum possible score is 10 and the maximum score is 50.

### 10–19 (Low Psychological Safety)

- Team members may be hesitant to speak up, fearing judgment or rejection.
- Mistakes may be punished rather than treated as learning opportunities.
- Likely impact: low engagement, reluctance to share ideas, and team tension.

**20–34 (Moderate Psychological Safety)**

- Some team members feel comfortable speaking up, but others may hesitate.
- The team may not always handle mistakes or disagreements constructively.
- Likely impact: cautious participation, occasional conflicts, and limited collaboration.

**35–50 (High Psychological Safety)**

- Team members feel safe sharing ideas, voicing concerns, and taking risks.
- Feedback is constructive, and mistakes are treated as opportunities to learn.
- Likely impact: strong collaboration, trust, innovation, and team success.

Psychological safety is the most important factor in team success and in ensuring that employees feel like they belong on the team. Once you figure out how psychologically safe your team feels, you can adjust to encourage everyone to do their best work.

## ONE-ON-ONE MEETINGS

One-on-one meetings serve as an opportunity to create a safe space with individual team members and to develop strong connections. These are purposeful touchpoints with an agenda designed by you and your team member to get to know them better.

In *Radical Candor*, author Kim Scott writes, "1:1s are

quiet, focused collaboration time for employees and bosses to connect. It's also the most important chance to hear from your employee, and it's their time, not yours."[8] In other words, the leader should talk less and listen more. It also means that these meetings have a high priority and should not be canceled or rescheduled unless it is necessary.

To be clear, a one-on-one meeting is not for project up-dates—you can get that in an email or a status meeting. It's also not a time for gossiping or whining or just making small talk.

The one-on-one meeting described here is important to build relationships and trust with team members. It allows employees to have a voice and feel heard, creating a sense of value. It's a safe space for specific conversations to learn about their career aspirations, what they like and don't like, and how you can be of help to them.

## PREPARING FOR THE ONE-ON-ONE MEETING

Successful one-on-one meetings begin with you and the team member reaching agreement on the purpose of the meeting, setting an agenda prior to each meeting, and establishing the frequency (usually thirty minutes to an hour weekly or biweek-ly). Documentation needed for the meeting is sent in advance.

The following is a sample meeting invite you can tailor for a one-on-one meeting:

> Hi [employee name],
> I would like to schedule a recurring time for us to
> have one-on-one meetings. We will use this time
> to learn more about each other and to connect on
> topics you'd like to discuss. These topics can include
> how you're feeling and how things are going, your

*career path, where you'd like additional support or resources, feedback for each other, and any questions you may have on your work.*

*I've scheduled our first one-on-one meeting for [date] at [time] for [length]. Let's plan to meet every [frequency of meetings] at [location].*

*If you have any questions, please let me know.*

*Also, please share any documents that you'd like to discuss in advance.*

*Thank you,*

*[Your name]*

This sets expectations for the one-on-one meeting and provides the participant with time to decide on topics they'd like to cover. It is also helpful for you to add topics to the agenda as they arise. One way to keep track of this is to have a file for each employee and add agenda items between one-on-one meetings.

## CONDUCTING THE ONE-ON-ONE MEETING

The one-on-one meeting is your time to build authentic relationships and rapport with team members. Be fully present—turn off your cell phone, shut down email and chats, and give your undivided attention. It's hard for a team member to feel important if you are distracted. If you're both working remotely, use video conferencing to help read body language. Listen carefully to what is being said instead of waiting for your turn to talk. Be prepared and don't rush through the meeting.

Take the time to learn about their interests and what's going on in their lives. Discussion points include the employee's well-being; career and personal goals and progress toward them; clarity around roles, assignments, and performance; areas for coaching and mentoring; and other nonurgent topics.

The following is an example of a reflection tool you can use to gauge how the team member is feeling. It's also a good way to generate questions for more probing. In the example, a low score for personal/professional growth would be a great opportunity to ask what would be needed to increase this score. Or if work culture is a 7, what would need to happen for it to be a 9 or 10? If a score has increased or decreased, you can ask what caused the change.

**How are you feeling about each of the areas below?**

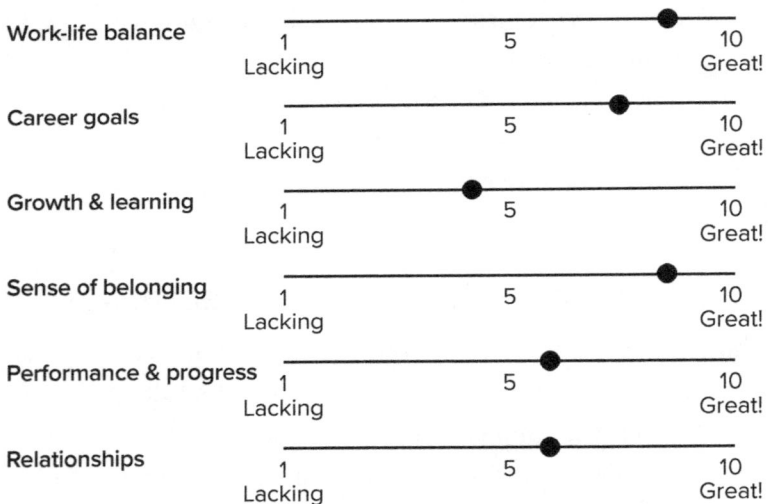

| Area | 1 Lacking | 5 | 10 Great! |
|------|-----------|---|-----------|
| Work-life balance | | | ● |
| Career goals | | | ● |
| Growth & learning | | ● | |
| Sense of belonging | | | ● |
| Performance & progress | | ● | |
| Relationships | | ● | |

A list of questions that may be used to help facilitate the one-on-one meeting includes the following:

- What are you most excited/worried about?
- What gives you the most job satisfaction?
- What would your ideal day look like?

- What are your current and long-term goals, and what skills do you need to develop to achieve them?
- If you could pick only one goal to accomplish in the next six months, what would it be?
- What can you do in the next month to make progress toward that goal?
- What obstacles are holding you back?
- How can I help?
- What gives you the most satisfaction at work?
- How have you been given feedback in the past that you felt was helpful?
- How do you like to receive feedback?
- What causes you the most stress?
- What typically frustrates you? How can I help when you're frustrated?
- What is your preferred means of communication?
- How can we make our one-on-one meetings better?

I'm not suggesting that you ask all these questions in one setting—that might feel more like an interrogation. Pick a few to start with and add your own. Give them time to reflect and answer questions thoughtfully. At the end of each one-on-one meeting, ask what you could do more of or less of to help them succeed in their role. From time to time, consider asking for feedback on your leadership.

The important takeaway is to make the one-on-one meetings a priority so that team members feel heard and understood. This goes a long way in building a trusting relationship.

## BUILD AN INCLUSIVE CULTURE

Leaders who are intentional about including all team members, regardless of differences related to race, ethnic backgrounds, gender, age, marital status, or sexual orientation, build a culture of team performance and innovation. Teams where everyone feels valued, heard, and respected are more engaged, better at solving problems, and more creative.

Reflect for a moment on how inclusive you are with your team. Here are a few questions to consider:

- Do I socialize with specific team members outside of work or in informal settings but not with others?
- Would team members say that I have favorites?
- Am I more lenient with mistakes or shortcomings for certain individuals compared to others?
- Do I give the same team members the most high-visibility or important assignments?
- Do I give challenging feedback to some team members while avoiding it with others?
- Am I holding everyone equally accountable for meeting deadlines and achieving results, or am I more lenient with some?
- Am I aware of any unconscious biases that may affect how I assign projects or responsibilities?
- Am I mindful of culture, gender, or other differences when planning team events or activities?
- Do I regularly check in with all team members?
- Do I acknowledge and respect the unique perspectives and experiences of each team member?
- Do I ask my team for feedback on how I can be more inclusive?

Did some of the questions give you insights into areas that might need attention?

Chapters 5 and 6 on emotional intelligence and biases go into more detail and provide tactics to help you become more aware of actions that may be interpreted as showing biases.

**Curiosity Questions for Inclusion.** Open-ended curiosity questions are a great tactic to use so that team members know you want ideas and feedback. Ask everyone for their thoughts, not just the ones who usually speak up. Asking questions that don't have just one correct answer creates an environment where everyone feels their input matters, encouraging participation from quieter or underrepresented voices.

Open-ended questions also signal to your team that you aren't looking for quick answers and that you want to understand differing viewpoints. Team members will feel more respected and appreciated, which, as you know, is key to inclusivity.

Leading questions, however, may discourage new perspectives or alternatives, causing a reluctance for employees to voice their opinions. For example, "Don't you agree that using a different solution is our best choice?" steers people toward a particular answer, potentially leading to a decision based on preconceived notions. Such questions imply that input from others is not important and that a decision has already been made. Another way to ask might be this: "What factors make a different solution a strong choice, and what other alternatives or factors should we consider?"

Ask open-ended curiosity questions and let team members know you value their perspectives. Here are a few examples of curiosity questions to consider:

- What am I missing?
- What other alternatives might we consider?
- Who has a different perspective?
- Do we have experience with this?
- Has anyone had experience with this in a different company?
- Are there similar situations from the past that we should be aware of?
- What potential risks or challenges do we have, and what contingency plans are needed?
- What questions should I be asking that I haven't?
- What ideas do you have that would allow us to be more efficient?

Open-ended curiosity questions signal to everyone that their ideas and perspectives are important and worthy of consideration. Encourage employees to speak up, even when it's unfavorable news, and remind them that they won't be blamed or reprimanded. This is an opportunity for you to lead by example by encouraging and appreciating team members who proactively communicate anticipated and known issues.

Creativity and innovation increase when individuals are comfortable bringing ideas and thoughts without fear of judgment or criticism. Collaboration becomes routine, and ideas are shared freely. Team members who trust you and one another are more likely to share challenges and to ask for assistance when needed.

## SUPPORT YOUR TEAM

Team support is understanding and addressing the needs of your employees. When team members feel supported, they are more engaged, productive, and committed to their work. Let's consider a few tactics.

**Provide Needed Resources.** Give team members the tools, training, and help needed for them to succeed in their roles. This builds confidence and offers growth and development opportunities.

**Be Approachable and Available.** Make sure you're available when employees need you. This could be through regular check-ins, an open-door policy, or setting aside time during one-on-one meetings. You could schedule a daily or weekly fifteen-minute office hour where any team member can drop in for a quick chat, either in person or online.

**Recognize Achievements.** Celebrating team and individual achievements boosts morale and reinforces the value of each person's contributions. An easy way to do this is to send out a team-wide email or to give a shout-out in a team meeting to recognize someone who went above and beyond what was expected.

**Actively Listen.** Few things show support as much as being genuinely interested in what a team member has to say. In team meetings, give each person an opportunity to speak, listen carefully, and respond thoughtfully to their input. Part 3 on effective communication goes into more detail on how to actively listen.

**Be Empathetic.** It's important to show emotional support to your team. Everyone faces challenges both at work and in their personal life. When you show empathy, it creates an environment where people feel cared for as humans, not just as workers. If a team member is going through a tough time, you may need to offer schedule flexibility or pick up some of their workload.

## INFLUENCING LIVES

The way you lead your team could likely be the difference between whether a parent attends family events or is frustrated by missing out yet again because of a poorly planned deadline. It could be the difference between burnout or engagement. High-performing teams or high attrition. Leadership expert John Maxwell says, "He who thinks he leads, but has no followers, is only taking a walk."

Great leaders don't *tell* people what to do; rather, they lead in ways that help them achieve results and that positively influence their lives. You are the mentor and guide who helps individuals navigate challenges and make informed decisions.

As a leader, you genuinely care about your team and their well-being. You help them succeed. You're there for them when they need you to be. Sure, part of your job is setting the direction and getting things done. It's a lot easier when you have employees who respect you and who are willing to do whatever it takes to help the team and the organization be successful.

Clayton M. Christensen, Harvard Business School professor and author, describes how he thinks about leaders:

> In my mind's eye, I saw one of my managers leave for work one morning with a relatively strong level of self-esteem. Then I pictured her driving home to

her family ten hours later, feeling unappreciated, frustrated, underutilized, and demeaned. I imagined how profoundly her lowered self-esteem affected the way she interacted with her children. The vision in my mind then fast-forwarded to another day, when she drove home with greater self-esteem—feeling that she had learned a lot, been recognized for achieving valuable things, and played a significant role in the success of some important initiatives. I then imagined how positively that affected her as a spouse and a parent. My conclusion: Management is the most noble of professions if it's practiced well.[9]

Your leadership has far-reaching effects outside the work environment. Work-life balance allows employees to prioritize family time, creating a more fulfilling home life. It reduces stress and burnout so that people can bring their best to both work and family.

CHAPTER FOUR

# MINDSET SHIFTS

**IN MY CONSULTING AND LEADERSHIP** development work with more than twenty-five companies from small to Fortune 50 across multiple industries and hundreds of people, I've observed the mindsets of many leaders. In some cases, the mindsets are spot-on, and the person is on a great trajectory. For others, the mindset is causing them to stagnate and has capped their career. For this chapter, I interviewed C-suite executives and leadership coaches to add their perspectives. Let's look more closely at the mindsets that leaders need to adopt to succeed in their career journey. Do you recognize yourself in any of these?

## FROM GO-TO EXPERT TO ACTIVE LISTENER AND FACILITATOR

A shift from being the go-to person who has the answers to the person who listens first and facilitates meetings to hear the ideas of others is a pivotal change for most leaders. As an expert, you were valued for having the right answers and for solving problems yourself. Leadership isn't about being center stage—it's about how you draw out the ideas, solutions, and contributions of others.

Teamwork: Everybody Doing Everything My Way was written on a coffee mug that a client gave Madison after a successful engagement within the company. At the time, Madison was a technical project manager who prided herself on her expertise. She liked being the go-to person when others had questions or complex projects to manage. She had completed the project on schedule and within budget and proudly displayed her coffee mug on her desk. Sure, there had been some bumps along the way and a few people on the team left. But the project was completed successfully.

Several years on, Madison's career moved her into executive roles in different organizations. Later, she pivoted to being an executive coach. During her interview for this book, she said, "When I was given the coffee mug at the end of the project, I took it as a compliment! Now I know that it was not. I was viewed as successful throughout my career but probably caused a lot of stress for those who worked for me. I missed several opportunities because there are a lot of other ways the work could've been done. The coffee mug is a reminder for me of being stuck in the skill-centric expert stage that doesn't serve leaders."

The mindset shift from being the smartest person in the room to being someone who is wiser and understands the role of listening and allowing others to bring ideas forward is challenging for many leaders and is one of the most common problems that hold leaders back.

Pranav, the CTO and CEO of several product companies, shared his perspective. "I have had to work hard at being a better listener and not needing to pile on to everyone's ideas. It's easy to get sucked into the I-need-to-have-all-the-good-ideas mindset or the I-need-to-have-something-to-add-to-that-great-idea leadership style. As I became more acutely aware of my knowledge and skill gaps, I started to better leverage my teams and resources. This has been a true force multiplier for my management style, as now I spend more time ensuring that my teams have the resources and focus they need to be successful."

This mindset shift isn't one that only new or mid-level leaders need to make. It's a problem for senior-level leaders and executives as well.

Christopher, a senior HR leader, shared his perspective on the challenge he sees with high achievers. "I think high-potential people sometimes struggle with transitioning from being high achievers on an individual level to recognizing that their success is tied to the success of their teams. This shift involves learning to trust, partner, and focus on empowering others rather than trying to do everything themselves, their way. This is a particularly difficult balance, as high-potential individuals are often looking to showcase and be recognized for their efforts and skills, which often equates to promotional opportunities."

He described the conversation in an executive meeting he had recently attended to review high-potential leaders in the company for additional development and promotion. "We have a director, Ryan, who has been with the company for several years and who has been pushing for a promotion. He gets results, but his 360 review pointed out that he was a my-way-or-the-highway kind of leader. The CEO said that his sharp elbows and HR complaints were not the type of leadership the company wanted and that unless he changed, he needed to look elsewhere for employment. I've provided coaching to Ryan, but whether he can change remains to be seen."

Consider this for a minute. Ryan thinks he is ready for his

next promotion. The CEO is ready to terminate him.

At some point in your career, you'll need to transition from wanting to be the smartest person in the room to becoming the most attentive listener if you want to continue progressing. Your ability to listen, understand, and collaborate will ultimately outweigh the do-it-my-way results you've achieved in the past.

The transition to being a great listener doesn't mean you are passive. You still need to facilitate discussions and ask insightful questions to extract the most valuable insights. It may be hard at first, especially if you default to giving answers instead of eliciting them. It's a mindset shift that will serve you well, especially as you progress to higher levels of leadership. Once I learned this and started asking others for their ideas, I was amazed by the creativity they brought to the conversation. People proposed solutions that I would never have thought of and that were better ways to approach the problem than my ideas.

No one leader can have all the right answers, especially in today's complex business environments. The collective intellectual horsepower that comes with actively listening to everyone's ideas is key to delivering the best solutions.

Chapter 6 includes tactics for improving self-awareness, and chapter 7 provides tips and strategies for honing active listening skills.

## FROM PERSONAL PERFORMANCE TO TEAM RECOGNITION

Once you move into a leadership role, it's time to shift the spotlight from yourself to your team and to recognize team wins, collective contributions, and individual efforts that drive the outcomes. For some, this is a hard mindset shift to make, especially because most people are measured on individual achievements and contributions early in their careers.

Maria, a mid-level manager, described her boss. "Victor takes credit for everything. He asked me to sit in on a presentation in case questions came up but not to say anything. During the meeting, he took credit for an approach that I had suggested and also for a fix that another team member had implemented. It was so frustrating hearing him talk about 'my approach, my fix, my presentation' without giving anyone on the team any credit." I asked Maria if she had given any presentations. "No. I asked Victor if either I or others on the team could handle some of the presentations for a learning experience, but he cut me off and said that he needed to be the point of contact."

Maria left her role. "Working for Victor was a different kind of learning experience for me. He taught me what not to do. With my teams today, I give them credit for everything. They lead presentations, and we help each other."

Once you're a leader, your effectiveness is no longer defined by what you personally accomplish but by the growth, success, and results of your team.

Imagine for a minute how demoralizing it is to work hard and then have your manager take credit for it. Maybe it's happened to you. Now imagine how uplifting it feels when you've been recognized for your hard work.

## FROM DOING TO DELEGATING

Another critical mindset shift a leader often needs to make is that of transitioning from doing the work to delegating it effectively. This shift means trusting others to execute tasks and ensuring that they are equipped with the knowledge, training, and tools to succeed. This change is harder for some leaders than for others.

Maddie, a coaching client, said, "I want things done correctly, and I spend a lot of time making sure my team knows how to do things." More than fifty people reported into her department, five of whom were direct reports. Maddie's 360 review results confirmed that she indeed wanted things done well, but that didn't translate into favorable ratings. Comments included feedback like this: "I feel like I am micromanaged. Maddie wants to tell me how to do every little thing, and I already know how to do my job"; "Maddie is a micromanager. Several of us feel like we have better ways to do things, but it's always her way. She would be a better manager if she'd give us more autonomy. She's always in the weeds instead of letting me figure things out"; "Maddie doesn't have one-on-one meetings with me very often, probably because she is so busy all the time."

When Maddie and I met to review her 360 results, she was taken aback by the comments. She put in long hours and cared about her team members and their well-being. She sat quietly for a bit, reflecting on the micromanager comments. "Wow, this is really surprising. I didn't realize that my team felt this way about me. I have some work to do, and I'm going to need your help. I thought that making sure we were doing things right was a good thing."

Let's be clear: Doing things correctly *is* a good thing, but you don't need to be a micromanager to make that happen. After a few coaching sessions, Maddie was able to shift her mindset and started to delegate more and focus on outcomes instead of micromanaging. She said, "It's actually liberating to let go of the need to be in the weeds and to trust people to do the job. It was hard at first but got easier with practice. It's not always how I would do it, but the outcomes are the same.

I have more time now for strategy and planning. My direct reports have noticed the change and thanked me."

Maybe you were the best developer who wrote the cleanest code, the underwriter who knew all the legalities of different types of loan or insurance claims, the compliance analyst who had federal regulations committed to memory, the analyst who could look at data or situations and interpret downstream effects—whatever you did, you were the best. You were the go-to expert. Your expertise likely played a big role in your promotion.

As you gain more responsibility in your leadership role, the amount of time you spend in meetings increases. If you don't learn to delegate, you need to work more hours to keep up with the workload—a recipe for personal disaster and professional doom.

Keep in mind that the earlier hard work and results that got you the promotion may also be your Achilles' heel. It's easy to get caught in this trap. Delegation isn't about relinquishing control; it's about amplifying results through others. Chapter 10 provides reasons why some people struggle to delegate and offers guidance on how to successfully assign work to help make this mindset shift.

## FROM PERFECTIONIST TO PROGRESS

We sometimes think about perfectionism as a measure of our high standards, which is a good thing in the right situations, like ensuring that payroll is accurate and that compliance requirements are met or in areas where loss of lives could occur. But in general, as a leader, your focus needs to shift from one of perfection to one of progress. This doesn't mean settling for mediocrity; it means recognizing when a task meets the necessary standards and trusting your team to move forward.

Chen, a highly respected CIO of a multibillion-dollar energy company, shared this with me: "Earlier in my career, I was very focused on perfecting tasks and projects, but as I progressed, I realized that leadership is more about setting a vision, empowering others, and making strategic decisions that align with long-term goals. This allowed me to understand the power of the team and to delegate more effectively to prioritize actions that drive the most value, rather than getting caught up in the details. This also forced me to ensure that the team or teams were moving and progressing along the strategy that we had set forward. The ability to slow down, review progress, and chart the future doesn't happen without intentionally making the time and space for that reflection."

Let's face it: As a leader, you don't get the easy problems; you get the hard ones. And the higher up you are, the more challenging the problems become. The time required to gather all the data may cause a delay that results in lost opportunities.

Liz, a state agency executive, said, "When you think you need to have all the details before making a decision, you delay it. Then you're deciding to not make a decision by default." She continued, "I tell my teams we have to make a decision based on the information we have right now. If something changes, we'll make adjustments when needed."

This mindset shift may be hard to make if you have high standards and are meticulous about details. It can be unsettling if you equate control with success. Maybe you're concerned that if you make a mistake, it will reflect poorly on you. The shift to a progress over perfection mindset requires you to accept that not every decision will be right. One of Liz's favorite quotes is this: "Nothing is ever as good as or as bad as originally thought."

In leadership roles, ambiguity is often the norm, and decisions are made based on incomplete information instead of on the certainty you'd like to have. Reframe the perfectionist mindset. Instead of focusing on perfect outcomes, think about making progress toward larger goals. Every decision, even if imperfect, moves the work forward. Think of mistakes as growth opportunities instead of as failures.

Chapter 12 provides more information on decision-making.

## FROM IDEAS TO BUSINESS OUTCOMES

It's important to generate ideas but even more important to ensure that ideas align with the organization's goals.

Pranav, the CTO/CEO from earlier, said, "One of the biggest changes I had to make from a mindset shift perspective was the notion of always thinking about business outcomes first over a good idea. Spend time on why we need to do something and its value to the business. Don't get pulled into how we will do it as soon as someone comes up with an idea.

"I step out every once in a while and make sure our plans and progress are aligned to the original thesis of why we are doing something."

How often do you see a new gadget, start thinking about how you'll use it, and then buy it online for next-day delivery? We believe something is a great idea and then start looking for ways to put it to use instead of understanding what is really needed.

Do you start thinking about how you and your team can implement a cool new idea before you know if it's aligned to organizational goals and outcomes? Chapter 13 provides a framework you can use for goal setting and prioritizing strategies.

## FROM TACTICAL TO STRATEGIC THINKING

Tactical thinking is useful for day-to-day operational activities but doesn't serve you well in a leadership role. Instead of being a problem solver, you now need to be the opportunity and problem forecaster.

Strategic thinking requires a broader view across the team, department, and organization, with a longer-term perspective. Chen also said, "A critical mindset shift for my leadership journey was moving from a focus on doing things right to doing the right things. I had to think much bigger picture and consider the right things for the department, my peers, and our stakeholders. I went from making work assignments based on what I was given to setting a vision and goals for my teams that aligned with the organization's overall direction."

Liz was unsure of how to navigate the transition of moving from tactical to strategic. She feared that if her manager asked her for details, she wouldn't know the answers. She said, "I initially felt a need to be more tactical and to know the details of the work my teams were doing. I was drowning with this approach with the eighty projects I was responsible for. I had to change how I was thinking. I needed to know the latest project status at a high level, but I didn't need all the details. I also learned that it was OK to say, 'Let me find out the answer to that for you.'"

Maybe you're wondering what it means to be *more strategic*. I find in my coaching that most leaders ask this question. Chapter 13 provides information on strategy, goal setting, and alignment, and chapter 8 has more detail on communicating with executives.

## MINDSET SHIFT PERSONAL ASSESSMENT

How well you make the needed mindset shifts as you progress in your leadership role will determine your success. Next is a personal assessment you can do to see what you have mastered and where you may need to make changes.

Rate each of the following statements using this scale:

1 = Strongly Disagree
2 = Disagree
3 = Neutral
4 = Agree
5 = Strongly Agree

Total your scores for each mindset shift and refer to the interpretation guide to understand your results.

| MINDSET SHIFT PERSONAL ASSESSMENT | |
|---|---|
| **From Go-to Expert to Active Listener and Facilitator** | **Rating** |
| I prioritize listening to others' ideas over sharing my own expertise. | |
| I create opportunities for team members to contribute and lead discussions. | |
| I remain open and receptive when others' ideas differ from my own. | |

| | |
|---|---|
| I actively ensure that all voices are heard during team interactions. | |
| I feel comfortable allowing others to lead conversations or decisions. | |
| **Score** | |
| **From Personal Performance to Team Recognition** | **Rating** |
| I celebrate team achievements more than individual contributions. | |
| I consistently share credit for successes with my team. | |
| I emphasize the value of teamwork over individual accomplishments. | |
| I support and encourage team members who excel, even when they outperform me. | |
| I create opportunities for my team to show-case their work and be recognized. | |
| **Score** | |

| From Doing to Delegating | Rating |
|---|---|
| I feel confident delegating important tasks to others. | |
| I carefully decide what tasks should be delegated based on team strengths and priorities. | |
| I provide clear instructions and resources when delegating responsibilities. | |
| I follow up with team members to offer support without micromanaging. | |
| I use systems to track delegated work and ensure accountability. | |
| **Score** | |

| From Perfectionist to Progress | Rating |
|---|---|
| I know when a task is complete and ready to move forward. | |
| I accept minor imperfections if they don't affect the overall outcome. | |
| I avoid letting the pursuit of perfection delay progress or decisions. | |

| | |
|---|---|
| I encourage my team to prioritize delivering value over achieving perfection. | |
| I balance maintaining high standards with setting realistic expectations. | |
| **Score** | |

| **From Ideas to Business Outcomes** | **Rating** |
|---|---|
| When I hear a new idea, my first instinct is to evaluate its alignment with business goals before considering how to implement it. | |
| I ensure that every new project or initiative is clearly linked to measurable business outcomes before investing time and resources. | |
| I focus on defining the "why" behind an idea and its value to the business before thinking about the execution details. | |
| I regularly step back to reassess whether current projects and work efforts are still aligned with their original purpose and expected business outcomes. | |

| | |
|---|---|
| I resist the urge to pursue new tools, technologies, or strategies simply because they are exciting; instead, I adopt them when they clearly solve a business need. | |
| **Score** | |

| **From Tactical to Strategic** | Rating |
|---|---|
| I dedicate sufficient time to long-term planning and strategy. | |
| I regularly align my daily activities with broader organizational goals. | |
| I delegate tactical tasks to focus on strategic priorities. | |
| I evaluate the long-term effect of my decisions and actions. | |
| I balance addressing immediate needs with maintaining a vision for the future. | |
| **Score** | |

Scoring interpretation for each mindset shift:

- **5 to 15:** Mindset shifts may need significant attention. Reflect on ways to actively work on this area.

- **16 to 20:** You are making progress but may still benefit from a more consistent application of this mindset.

- **21 to 25:** You have a strong grasp of this mindset shift and are likely applying it effectively in your leadership.

Leadership starts with how you think. Making the shift from being an individual contributor to a first-time leader or from a first-time leader to a senior leader isn't just about learning new skills—it's also about being aware of your mindset and the need to make changes along the way. As a leader, your focus must move from your own performance (one person) to the growth and success of your team (a multiple).

You'll need to get comfortable with more ambiguity, learn to delegate, and start thinking more strategically. These shifts won't happen overnight, but they are essential if you want to succeed as a leader. By being intentional about your mindset and making these changes, you set yourself and your team up for long-term success. Leadership isn't just a title—it's a way of thinking that allows you to earn trust, deliver results, and change lives.

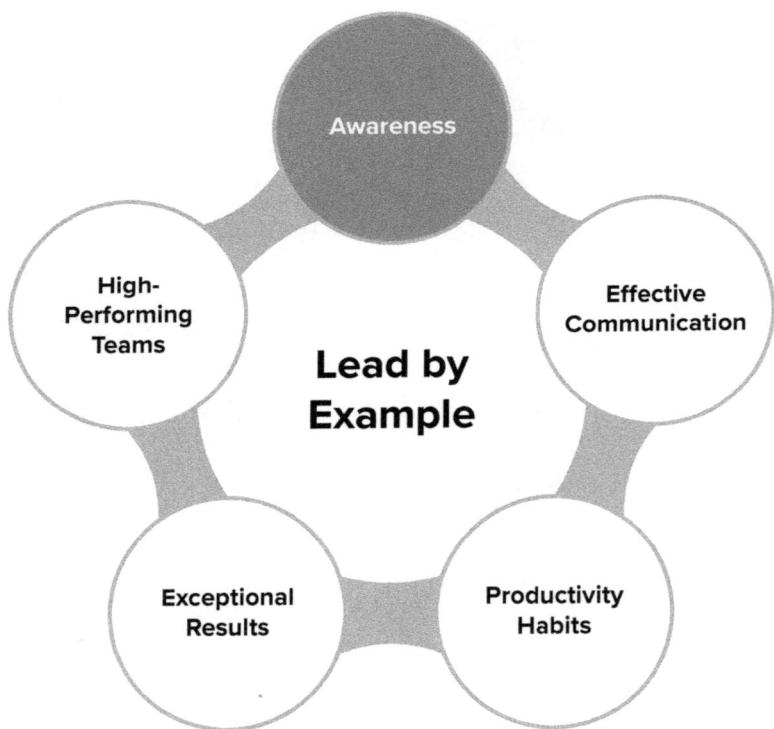

Awareness

High-Performing Teams

Effective Communication

Lead by Example

Exceptional Results

Productivity Habits

# PART TWO

## AWARENESS

Between stimulus and response, there is a space.
In that space is our power to choose our response.
In our response lies our growth and our freedom.

**—VIKTOR FRANKL**

**WE ALL BRING OUR OWN PERSONAL EXPERIENCES,** values, and
cultural backgrounds to the workplace that influence how we
think, communicate, and act. While beliefs provide a sense
of stability, they can also lead to unconscious biases—auto-
matic judgments that impact hiring, communications, and
decision-making, often without us realizing it.

As a leader, it's not enough to be aware of your own biases;
you must also recognize and address those within your teams.
Understanding how the brain processes information—often by
filtering and simplifying complex details—can help challenge

assumptions, improve collaboration with diverse perspectives, and create a more inclusive and productive work environment.

Beyond recognizing biases, you must also develop emotional intelligence to help you manage the day-to-day challenges more effectively. Leaders with high self-awareness, self-management, social awareness, and relationship management can regulate their emotions, communicate effectively, and build trust with their teams. Without it, even the most well-intentioned leaders struggle to connect with their people, handle conflicts, or get results.

Cognitive and emotional awareness helps you make better decisions, build stronger teams, and create a culture of trust and collaboration.

CHAPTER FIVE

# BELIEFS, BRAIN SCIENCE, AND BIASES

**"GIRLS CAN'T FLY AIRPLANES,"** said Uncle Bud. We were at my parents' house celebrating Thanksgiving, and he had asked where my car was. I told him that I had flown my plane to the local airport. He didn't believe me until my parents backed me up.

"If girls can't fly airplanes," I asked him, "how am I going to get home?"

His belief that the ability to fly airplanes was limited to the male gender doesn't seem all that far-fetched if you consider some of the things that other people believe. According to survey results reported in *Conspiracy vs. Science: A Survey of U.S. Public Beliefs,* when respondents were presented with the statement "NASA did not land on the moon," 12 percent agreed, 17 percent were unsure, and 71 percent disagreed. When given the statement "The Earth is flat, not round," 10 percent agreed, 9 percent were unsure, and 80 percent disagreed. Only 83 percent agreed that the earth revolves around the sun.[1]

Here are four important things to remember when it comes to beliefs:

1. Unless something is based on a law of nature, it is simply a shared belief. Even with scientific proof, some people continue to believe otherwise.
2. If someone's belief isn't based on logic, you aren't going to change it with logic. You'll save yourself a lot of time if you keep this in mind and instead find ways to work with the belief or around it.
3. You and everyone you know likely have beliefs that are untrue.
4. Your beliefs subconsciously guide your actions and may conflict with others who have different beliefs.

Read those four statements again and let them sink in. It's taken me a long time to fully grasp the effect of belief systems. Dr. Wayne Dyer, author and motivational speaker, said this: "Our suffering is caused by the mind—a mind that insists on having preferences and won't allow others to be just as they are."

As a leader, you will encounter many people who have different beliefs and biases. Awareness helps you successfully navigate your own beliefs and those of others.

A belief system is a deeply ingrained set of values, principles, and assumptions that include biases you might not realize you have. It's the way you see the world through perceiving, understanding, and interpreting things that happen. For example, you know from my story in chapter 1 that I believed my successful career playbook was to get a good education and to work hard. This belief was challenged when I was planning to lead a book study with my team. I asked them to read a chapter a week and be prepared to share key takeaways in our weekly meeting. One of the team members, Connor, immediately said, "When, exactly, do you expect me to read this book? I play golf after work." It hadn't occurred to me that not everyone wanted to improve themselves by reading a book. I made the book study optional so that no one felt pressured to read outside business hours.

Different beliefs are all around. You may have someone on your team who believes that failing at a task is a personal shortcoming to be avoided at all costs, while you believe that it is a necessary part of learning. Perhaps you'd like team members to provide constructive feedback regularly to you, but some of them believe that questioning authority should be discouraged. Or you believe that conflict is a healthy way to clear up misunderstandings, while others believe that conflict should be avoided at all costs to maintain peace.

You can see how everyone's unique belief system makes leading others a challenge. The good news is that although we are all different, we are predictably different. You'll learn more about that shortly in the discussion on personality types.

Let's look at a few ways our brain comes into play.

## FIGHT, FLIGHT, OR FREEZE

Your manager sends a text message that reads: "I need ten minutes with you before the end of the day." What's the first thing that pops into your mind? It's unlikely your reaction will be, *How exciting! I'm sure it's good news.* Typically, the assumption is that something bad is about to happen, and you do a quick memory scan for anything you did that might get you in trouble.

You can thank the part of the brain known as the amygdala, which determines fight, flight, or freeze responses when we face uncertainty, risk, or danger. This was a handy response when survival depended on avoiding saber-tooth tigers, but today's dangers are different. The saber-tooth tiger might be the fears around not being accepted, a job change that requires new skills, a fear of failing, looking bad in front of team members or peers, or layoff concerns.

Keep this in mind when you send a quick text or an email to someone asking for a meeting. Provide context so that they don't needlessly worry. If the text you received from your manager was, "I need ten minutes with you before the end of the day to go over the report you sent," you probably wouldn't experience any anxiety. Be aware that cryptic text messages or emails may put someone on high alert or add to their stress.

The amygdala, which assumes something is dangerous, is hardwired to cause us to avoid risks. It tries to shut down anything that moves us out of our comfort zone. You need to understand this when confronting challenges that require different ways of working. When people are reluctant to learn a new system or change direction, or when you find that people are sabotaging a new initiative, now you know why. The amygdala is signaling, *Danger! Danger! Stay in the comfort zone!* You will need to explain the need for change and provide reassurances that the necessary training and support will be provided.

## INFORMATION OVERLOAD

The brain is bombarded by more than eleven million bits of information per second, but it can handle about fifty.[2] Yes, five zero. The reticular activating system (RAS), a bundle of nerves located in the brain stem, plays a role in filtering what information gets through to your brain. Without the RAS, we wouldn't be able to filter out the information we don't need. Driving a car would be impossible (or at least dangerous) if you had to process eleven million pieces of information per second while on the road.

Why is this important for you to know as a leader? The RAS filters out most information we are exposed to, but it does so in a way that supports our beliefs and interests. We see what we want to see or what we are looking for. For example, if you have already made up your mind that a particular solution is the best, your RAS may filter out innovative ideas from team members. You may not be as receptive to alternative solutions.

By focusing on information that supports our beliefs, the RAS can lead to self-fulfilling prophecies. The RAS ensures that only belief-affirming information enters our conscious awareness while potentially useful, contradictory information is ignored. An example of this would be if a leader believes a team member is ineffective, the RAS may filter out instances in which the person is doing a good job. This reinforces the leader's negative perception and potentially affects how the leader treats that employee.

You should be seeing that the RAS is a big contributor to biases, which is covered later in this chapter.

Fortunately, the brain's prefrontal cortex (PFC) helps balance the emotional responses of the RAS and the amygdala. It is the reasoning part of the brain that helps you make decisions, solve problems, set goals, reason, and choose appropriate responses.

In *Your Brain at Work*, author David Rock points out that the PFC, although critical to our survival, also has big limitations. It was the last area of our brain to evolve and takes up only 4 to 5 percent of the brain's volume. "To put these limitations in perspective, imagine that the processing resources for holding thoughts in our minds would be roughly equivalent to the value of the coins in your pocket right now.

If this were so, the processing power of the rest of your brain would be roughly equivalent to the entire US economy (perhaps before the financial crisis of 2008)." Rock refers to the PFC as the $0.10 computer and the subconscious mind as the $100 million computer.[3]

The good news is that we have a reasoning area in our brain to help balance the filtered information and the emotional responses. The bad news is that the role of the PFC is tiny in comparison to what goes on in our subconscious.

Why should you care about this? Because we need to be aware of the limitations we have when it comes to our emotions and our behaviors. We can't help but have biases.

## WE ARE EMOTIONAL
## BEFORE WE ARE RATIONAL

The five senses (see, hear, smell, taste, and touch) come in through the spinal cord/brain stem. Information sent from our senses goes first through the RAS, where it likely is filtered by what our subconscious perceives as the most aligned with beliefs. Then the limbic (emotional) system in the amygdala determines whether a fight, flight, or freeze response is required. If not, the information finally makes it to the PFC, where reasoning and thinking take place.

This brain science lesson is important to you for several reasons as you advance as a leader. First and foremost, if your team is in a stressful situation, the amygdala may trigger a fight, flight, or freeze response before the rational PFC can fully assess the situation. Team members may have a knee-jerk reaction that leads to conflict, avoidance, or inaction. Keep high stress to a minimum. This ties in to creating a psychologically safe work environment.

## We Are Emotional Before We Are Rational

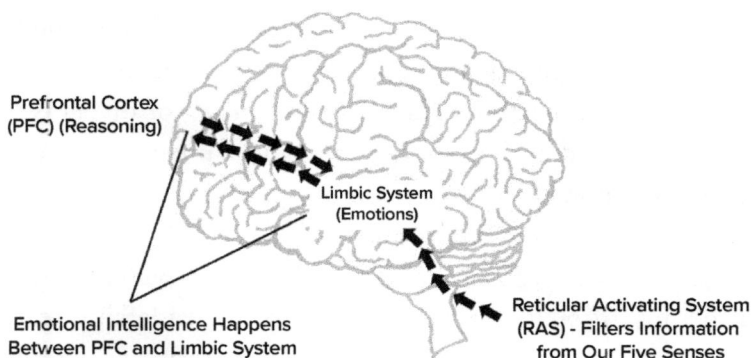

Prefrontal Cortex
(PFC) (Reasoning)

Limbic System
(Emotions)

Emotional Intelligence Happens
Between PFC and Limbic System

Reticular Activating System
(RAS) - Filters Information
from Our Five Senses

Second, as mentioned earlier, the RAS filters out information that doesn't align with a person's beliefs and experiences. This filtering may cause you to unconsciously ignore information that doesn't fit your preconceived notions.

Constructive feedback can trigger a storm of defensive emotions. You want to deliver feedback in a way that reduces emotional triggers, framing it to focus on how to help the person improve. This is covered in more detail in part 3 on effective communication.

As a leader, part of your job is problem-solving. Are you using we've-always-done-it-this-way thinking, or are you considering innovative and creative ideas? If so, your amygdala is working to keep you in your comfort zone.

Let's take a deeper look at the biases caused by beliefs and how our brain works.

## BIASES ARE NATURAL AND UNIVERSAL

Several years ago, I was in a client meeting with about ten people from my company and the same number from the client side. The attendees were senior leaders in both organizations. We sat on one side of the large conference table, facing the client. The CEO, Ravi, walked in, looked around, and said to our senior vice president, "Josh, why do you have only one woman in this meeting? Have you not heard of diversity?" Ravi's team had a good mix of men and women, white and people of color. Josh's team comprised white men with the exception of me, a white woman.

Later that day, Josh said to me, "I've never paid attention to the mix of people in meetings or in the leadership team until Ravi pointed it out. He really takes it seriously. I think we need to do a better job at our company."

There is a reason why things like this are overlooked.

Biases are formed as a cognitive shortcut. In the preceding section, we learned that we would have perpetual information overload if the RAS didn't filter the millions of pieces of information that bombard our brain each second. Our brain relies on shortcuts, called heuristics, to make judgments and decisions efficiently. For example, we don't need to know every detail about our surroundings when driving a car. We focus on the things that are most important, such as highway signs, roadways, speed traps, and other cars.

The RAS helps with these mental shortcuts but may also be flawed by filtering out or minimizing the importance of information that doesn't align with our subconscious mind and beliefs. The resulting mental shortcuts lead to inaccurate or skewed judgments where fairness and objectivity are critical.

Given the overwhelming amount of information leaders must process on a daily basis, ranging from team dynamics to strategic decisions, biases often emerge when the brain is on cognitive overload. In this moment, the brain defaults to the mental shortcuts, which may unconsciously influence decision-making. You may unknowingly rely on biases to make quick judgments about people, situations, or choices.

As a leader, you must recognize that everyone has biases; no one is immune based on their upbringing, education, or life experiences. Biases are not inherently malicious or intentional, but they can affect how you make critical decisions, treat people, or evaluate team member performance.

These biases can have a wide-ranging effect. You may ignore talented individuals because your bias tells you that someone who looks or acts in a certain way isn't a good fit for a role. You may give more attention or opportunities to people who are more aligned with your beliefs while unintentionally neglecting others. A negative team environment may be created if certain team members feel undervalued or excluded, which reduces their engagement, creativity, and performance. You may unconsciously promote someone or give higher performance ratings to those who fit a preconceived notion of success.

Let's examine common examples of unconscious biases in the workplace and the techniques to mitigate them.

## UNCONSCIOUS BIASES

An unconscious bias is one that operates outside your conscious awareness and that influences decisions without you realizing it. Let's look at several examples.

### Workplace Bias

I was the only woman in a meeting one day when Nathan, a senior manager, walked in, looked around, and said, "We don't have any coffee in here," then stared at me.

I replied, "I don't drink coffee, so you'll need to get it yourself." He quickly realized his mistake, apologized, and sheepishly went to get coffee for the group. After that, Nathan made it a point to either get coffee himself or ask another man to do it.

Biases in the workplace are common and often unconscious. We see job postings with equal opportunity statements that the company will not discriminate based on gender identity, color, age, sex, disability, national origin, race, religion, sexual orientation, or veteran status. Yet it happens frequently. Sometimes it's just a matter of bringing a behavior to someone's attention, like with Nathan. They aren't aware that their behavior reflects a bias.

Many people may not feel comfortable calling someone out. This is where you as the leader must work on their behalf and lead by example.

People sometimes believe that some roles are better suited for one gender over another. Researchers Stefanie K. Johnson and Jessica F. Kirk conducted a study on the application process for research time at the Hubble Space Telescope from 2001 to 2018, using data from 15,545 applicants. Only 18 percent of the females who submitted research proposals were accepted, although 23 percent of the applications were submitted by women. The evaluation committee decided to anonymize the application process, removing all personally identifiable information. The number increased from 18 percent to 30 percent with this change.[4]

Another study evaluating men and women who performed for orchestra auditions showed that 20 percent more women were chosen when the auditions were conducted blindly and the musician played behind a curtain than when the musician was visible to the judges.[5]

Similar to gender bias, names associated with ethnicity and race on a résumé can cause unconscious bias. According to a study in the *American Economic Review*, people with ethnic-sounding names are 50 percent less likely to be called for a job than people with Caucasian names.[6] A study conducted in 2021 to expand the previous study found that a typical employer called back the presumably white applicant 9 percent more than Black ones, with the worst offenders favoring white applicants by 24 percent.[7] This unconscious bias may cause you to exclude highly qualified candidates for positions.

It's not just the hiring process where gender and racial biases can creep in. Sometimes work assignments are made based on gender. For example, if travel is required, the assignment may be given to a man over a woman, thinking that the woman needs to care for children at home. Or more mundane work is given to women and minorities—like finding coffee for a meeting.

Promotions still favor men. A 2024 study conducted by LeanIn.org and McKinsey analyzed information from 281 organizations, surveying more than 15,000 employees and 280 HR leaders. At the manager level, 40 percent are women (27 percent white, 10 percent women of color). Men comprise 49 percent, with 41 percent white men and 18 percent men of color. The disparity becomes more pronounced in the senior manager, vice president, senior vice president, and C-suite levels. At the senior vice president level, 58 percent are white men, 13 percent are men of color, 22 percent are white women, and 6 percent are women of color.[8]

Research done by the Society for Human Resource Management in 2023 showed that 30 percent of workers in the United States say they have felt unfairly treated due to their age at some point in their career. Additional findings in the report revealed that older people are more likely to be perceived as not competent with technology (49 percent), resistant to new ways of doing things (38 percent), and stubborn or grumpy (48 percent).[9]

Numerous studies and decades of research have found that diverse teams tend to think more logically, are more creative, and are better at identifying errors in thinking.

How can you ensure that you aren't biased?

The first step is recognizing that we all have biases. Acknowledging this and being aware of it means that you can intentionally start paying closer attention to how you interact with people of all backgrounds.

Second, question your beliefs. Ask yourself why you believe something and whether you're open to the opinions of others.

The following bias self-assessment may help you uncover a few areas where you can improve. Be sure to answer the questions that relate to evidence of your response. How would your team answer these questions about you?

Use the following scale:

- 1 = Never
- 2 = Rarely
- 3 = Sometimes
- 4 = Often
- 5 = Always

| # | QUESTION | SCORE |
|---|----------|-------|
| 1 | Do I treat all team members equally in terms of recognition, feedback, and opportunities for growth, regardless of their background, appearance, or personal characteristics?<br><br>*What specific examples demonstrate fairness and inclusivity in my actions?* | |
| 2 | Do I make a conscious effort to evaluate someone's abilities, potential, and leadership style based on their skills and contributions rather than on any preconceived notions?<br><br>*How do I ensure that this effort is consistent?* | |
| 3 | Do I actively seek diverse perspectives when making decisions, ensuring input from individuals with varying backgrounds, experiences, and viewpoints?<br><br>*What steps have I taken to include these voices?* | |

| 4 | Do I hold all employees to the same standard when it comes to performance evaluations and accountability, regardless of their background or personal characteristics?<br><br>*Are my evaluations free from unintentional bias?* | |
| --- | --- | --- |
| 5 | Do I intentionally distribute challenging assignments or high-visibility projects equitably across team members?<br><br>*What patterns exist in my choices?* | |
| 6 | Do I take the time to reflect on how my own background, experiences, or preferences might shape my expectations or evaluations of team members?<br><br>*How do I ensure objectivity?* | |
| 7 | Do I ensure that all team members feel heard and valued during discussions, regardless of their communication style, background, or perspective?<br><br>*How do I encourage open dialogue?* | |

| 8 | Do I evaluate job candidates based solely on their skills, experience, and potential contributions, ensuring that personal characteristics such as gender, age, race, or background do not influence my decisions?<br><br>*How do I ensure fairness and consistency throughout the hiring process?* | |
|---|---|---|
| 9 | Do I invest equally in the career development of all team members, ensuring that everyone has access to mentoring and growth opportunities?<br><br>*How do I track my efforts to ensure fairness?* | |
| 10 | Do I actively seek feedback from team members with different backgrounds, perspectives, or personal characteristics to ensure that my leadership is inclusive?<br><br>*How do I act on the feedback I receive?* | |
| | **Total Score** | |

Scoring interpretation:

- **10 to 19:** You may need to focus significantly on developing inclusive leadership practices. Consider seeking resources or training to improve.

- **20 to 29:** There are noticeable gaps in your efforts to lead inclusively. Reflect on specific areas for improvement and take action.

- **30 to 39:** You exhibit a solid effort in being inclusive but have areas where you can strengthen your practices.

- **40 to 50:** You demonstrate strong inclusivity and fairness in your leadership practices. Continue seeking feedback and refining your approach to maintain this standard.

Biases are a natural part of being human and don't define your intentions or values. What matters most is your willingness to acknowledge them and take steps to improve.

## Similarity (Me Too) Bias

The similarity bias shows a tendency for us to gravitate toward people who are similar to us, whether it's through shared hobbies, alma mater, or background. We are naturally more comfortable with people who think like we do and with whom we share similar beliefs. It's why we like certain sports teams, attend a specific church, or live in a particular neighborhood. However, a similarity bias could lead you to unconsciously hire and promote people who are most like you, leading to a lack of diversity and perceived favoritism.

One of my client companies took hiring similar people to a whole new level. I commented to Tom, the COO, that I had never seen so many similar last names in a company's email directory, especially the number of uncommon last names. He replied, "Let me explain. We hire people who grew up in the surrounding area and graduated from the local university. We marry someone who works here and, within a few years, have kids. When the kids grow up, we hire them. Some of us divorce our spouse and marry someone else at the company." I have firsthand knowledge that the success of an outside hire at that company resembled a body rejecting an organ. It seemed like things were going well for a short while, and then they weren't. I can also attest that the company culture was one of mediocrity and little innovation. Within a few months of my engagement, the company's executive leadership was replaced, and multiple offices were opened in larger cities and technology hubs.

Hiring people who are like you can lead to a team that lacks diversity, which in turn limits creativity, performance, and innovation. The team becomes an environment where like-minded individuals reinforce one another's views. This leads to groupthink, where teams fail to challenge assumptions or explore alternatives, ultimately limiting new ideas and critical thinking.

A way to overcome this bias is to intentionally expand your network to include people from different backgrounds, experiences, and perspectives. You can join networking groups or ask for feedback from people outside your immediate circle.

You can also use objective, measurable criteria to evaluate candidates during interviews, performance reviews, and promotions. This helps you make decisions based on qualifications, skills, and achievements instead of on personal affinity.

Using diverse hiring panels to interview candidates and to weigh in on candidate selection can ensure that candidates are evaluated fairly.

When assembling teams to work on projects, include members from diverse backgrounds for collaboration. This helps bring innovative ideas to the table and reduces the effects of similarity bias.

## Confirmation Bias

Confirmation bias is the tendency to search for and use information in a way that supports or reinforces one's established beliefs, values, and prejudices. People display this bias when they actively look for information that supports their views while ignoring what doesn't, or they choose to interpret ambiguous evidence as supporting their views. Sports fans, for example, will decide whether a referee made a good or bad call depending on the team they're rooting for.

At work, confirmation bias may influence you to omit information that doesn't align with your point of view or support the decision you want to make. Processing facts and multiple perspectives takes time and energy. The RAS prefers to select information that supports your beliefs and knowledge, and it's tempting to use this cognitive shortcut to make decisions faster. But such decisions can come with a significant price tag.

A blatant example of confirmation bias is that of political pundits. These individuals frame news stories in a way that supports their own political views. They cherry-pick data and selectively cite polls or anecdotes that align with their viewpoint while conveniently ignoring evidence that contradicts it. Do you tend to watch news stations that align with your political viewpoints and disregard others? Most people do. We want to enforce our beliefs by listening to people who agree with us.

It's likely that you play an important role when hiring new people to join your team. If you believed that only men could fly airplanes, as my uncle Bud did, the aviation industry would be missing out on thousands of talented pilots. There would be no need to keep searching for Amelia Earhart because she shouldn't have been flying a plane in the first place.

Confirmation bias is especially problematic because people cling to their beliefs even in the face of contradictory evidence. For example, Kodak, once the leader in photography, eventually filed for bankruptcy because their executives downplayed the significance of digital photography and doubled down on their belief that film was the future.

Lawrence, a client and vice president of a technology division, wanted to implement a data warehouse solution that would be used to provide analytics to sales and operations. This solution had been in place in his previous company and was widely used. He was convinced that it could be functional within two months, even though he was not involved in his prior company's implementation. He cited unrealistic vendor-provided completion dates and the earlier success. In my role as the project management office leader, I pushed back on the timeline, providing a detailed list of all the work that would need to be done and the resources required. He didn't believe that it would take more than two months, became more insistent that the vendor could deliver the solution, and moved the project to the top priority. No amount of information would change his mind. I listed the project as high risk and immediately showed the schedule and budget as red on the project dashboard that I presented monthly to executives. Every month, I would report the project status and Lawrence would make excuses or contradict what I said.

Months later, tens of thousands of dollars were spent above the original budget, and the solution was only partially implemented. Data errors caused inaccurate reporting. The sales and operations team lost confidence and went back to their manual reporting. The project was canceled.

Lawrence's confirmation bias cost not only tens of thousands of extra dollars but also his credibility within the company. No one enjoys working on projects like that one.

As we saw in the example of the client company I mentioned earlier, confirmation biases also occur in the hiring process. A recruiter or hiring manager may view candidates who graduated from Ivy League universities more favorably than others. You may subconsciously look for reasons to hire someone who went to your alma mater or who has similar interests to you. One of my clients told me that they liked to hire people who ran every morning because that meant they were more disciplined than people who didn't. Another leader described a similar bias for people who served in the military, believing they were more structured and disciplined and less likely to push back when given assignments.

Remember—unless it's a law of nature, it's just a belief, and this kind of thinking causes you to miss opportunities.

Biases in the workplace are numerous and far-reaching, often resulting in serious consequences for employees and the organization. From gender and racial biases to those based on age, sexual orientation, or disability, these unconscious tendencies can lead to inequitable treatment and missed opportunities. As a leader, you shape the culture of your team. By recognizing and addressing biases, you build trust, a sense of belonging, and a more inclusive and high-performing team.

# CHAPTER SIX

# EMOTIONAL INTELLIGENCE

**"LOOKS LIKE YOU'VE PUT ON SOME WEIGHT** since the last time I saw you," my dad said to one of my cousins whom we hadn't seen in a couple of years. She was stunned and speechless. I was aghast. My dad always had good intentions, but sometimes his social skills needed work. OK, that's an understatement. What he was thinking and what came out of his mouth were unfiltered and often a surprise.

You may be as horrified as I was when you read that, imagining how someone you know who struggles with their weight would feel. Yet we see and hear damaging words and actions in the workplace every day. We've all been in meetings in which two or three people like to hear themselves talk, cutting other people off, and it's nearly impossible to get a word in edgewise. Or the person who dismisses everyone else's ideas in favor of their own by rolling their eyes, crossing their arms, or looking disinterested. These dismissive behaviors can make a person's contributions feel unimportant and unworthy.

Sometimes a lack of awareness is a bit more subtle. In one of my coaching sessions, Andre was frustrated because he felt that the employees who worked in satellite offices such as his were often an afterthought. He said, "It feels like the good-ole'-boys club, except it's the corporate club. I joined a call yesterday, and my boss was telling others about how several of the guys had gone out to dinner the night before and how much fun they had. He does this all the time. I was getting chat messages during the call from others who were making jokes about the corporate clique. We don't get much recognition and are often passed over for training or promotions."

Andre's manager, Rick, had been hired into the headquarters office years ago and worked his way up to a senior director role. He was unaware that his conversations were causing an us-versus-them divide across his own team. This was a big blind spot for him. When I talked with Rick about this, he was surprised. "I thought I was connecting and building rapport with the team by talking about my personal life with other team members. I had no idea I was alienating people." He started traveling more to the satellite offices and made it a point to recognize everyone for their contributions.

Author Stephen Covey sums up the problem with this quote: "We judge ourselves by our intentions and others by their behavior." It's also true that we judge ourselves by our intentions and that others judge us by our actions. Rick had good intentions, but his actions caused him to be viewed poorly by his remote team members.

This disconnect highlights a critical gap that emotional intelligence aims to bridge—understanding and managing the impact of our actions on others.

## DEFINING EMOTIONAL INTELLIGENCE

Emotional intelligence (EI) is defined as "the ability to rec-ognize and understand emotions in yourself and others, and your ability to use this awareness to manage your behavior and relationships" by researchers Travis Bradberry and Jean Greaves, who authored the best-selling book *Emotional Intelligence 2.0* and founded the company TalentSmartEQ.[10] Unlike intelligence quotient (IQ), which focuses on reasoning, problem-solving, and analytical thinking, EI centers on emotional and interpersonal competencies that are important for leadership effectiveness.

The term emotional intelligence was first introduced in 1990 by two psychology professors, John D. Mayer of the University of New Hampshire and Peter Salovey of Yale. Daniel Goleman, often considered the foremost expert on EI, established its importance to business leadership in his 1995 book, *Emotional Intelligence*, and in his 1998 *Harvard Business Review* article, "What Makes a Leader." Since that time, hundreds of articles have been published based on extensive research throughout the years.

## THE IMPORTANCE OF EMOTIONAL INTELLIGENCE

TalentSmartEQ reports that people who have very high emotional intelligence make an average of $29,000 per year more than those who have low EI. It was also found to be the strongest predictor of performance, explaining 58 percent of success in all jobs. Ninety percent of top performers score high on EI while only 20 percent of low performers score high.[11] It's unlikely that anyone who scores low will become a top performer without significant effort to develop their emotional intelligence.

Reflect on these statistics for a minute. I had a decent IQ, worked hard, and got things done but was almost fired because of my low EI. I don't want this to happen to you, and neither do you. It's one of the reasons why you're reading this book.

Let's look at each of the four areas—self-awareness, self-management, social awareness, and relationship management—that comprise EI and the tactics for developing each.

## SELF-AWARENESS: THE FOUNDATION OF EMOTIONAL INTELLIGENCE

Self-awareness is the ability to recognize, understand, and regulate your actions, thoughts, or emotions. People with high self-awareness understand their strengths, beliefs, and limitations. They know how they feel, and self-awareness helps them understand why they feel that way. Chapter 5 highlighted ways to become aware of your biases, and this chapter builds on that.

Your paradigms and belief system affect your emotions. Children who grew up watching a parent react to stress with anger and yelling have that behavior programmed into their subconscious. It's natural for people to react in the ways they observed in their formative years, so they are likely to have a similar reaction to stress unless they become conscious of the reason and take action to change it.

You may tend to micromanage if you were raised by helicopter parents who were constantly checking on you. Micromanaging might feel normal to you but drives people nuts who want more autonomy in their work.

You can't change your behavior without awareness. A prerequisite for developing self-awareness is understanding how beliefs and emotions affect your reactions and behaviors. With this awareness, along with a desire to change, the intentional creation of new habits, and practice, you can learn to remain calm under stress, handle difficult situations rationally, and demonstrate leadership characteristics that make others want to follow you.

How does one become more self-aware? The first step is to acknowledge the need for self-awareness and want to make improvements.

## TACTICS FOR BECOMING MORE SELF-AWARE

Several tools are available to help you become more aware of how your beliefs and emotions are reflected in your actions. Let's look at a few of them.

### Personality Assessments

Personality profile assessments and questionnaires are useful tools to gain deeper insights into your behaviors, preferences, and tendencies. The two I have the most experience with are the DiSC and the Myers-Briggs Type Indicator (MBTI). I'll use my DiSC assessment to show you how it helped me develop self-awareness.

The DiSC assessment categorizes individuals into one of four behavioral styles: dominance, influence, steadiness, and conscientiousness. The figure that follows shows an overview of the categories and associated characteristics.

Based on my story in chapter 1, you might guess I scored highest in dominance (D). I also scored above the midline on conscientiousness (C). Thus, my personality style is DC. In general, people like me focus on results, prefer a direct communication style, make quick decisions, and like to be in charge.

## DiSC Overview

- Seeks control
- Decisive
- Direct
- Results-focused

- Positive
- Spontaneous
- Friendly
- Spotlight

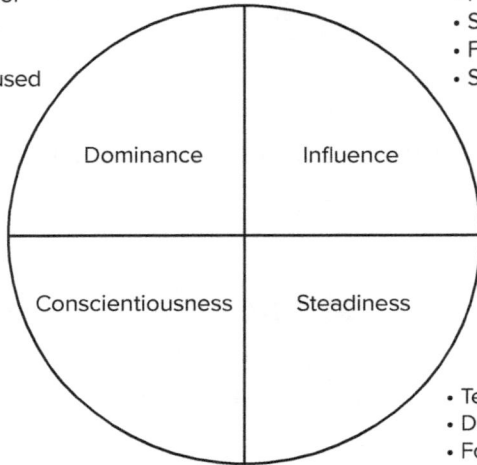

Dominance

Influence

Conscientiousness

Steadiness

- Compliant
- Analytical
- Planner
- Accuracy

- Team-oriented
- Detailed
- Follow-through
- Loyal

My tendencies are to analyze, plan the work, and then deliver excellent results. If results are the primary focus, these are good traits to have! However, with strengths come weaknesses, and the DiSC helped me uncover several blind spots.

Dominance personalities typically aren't great at details. They don't like the how-to questions—they prefer to focus on problems and results. The best way to communicate with us is summarized as follows: be brief, be bright, be gone.

For me, thinking about people first doesn't come naturally. Knowing this about myself allows me to understand why I start feeling frustrated when someone takes a long time to get to the point.

Ask your HR department if they offer personality assessments to employees. If so, complete it and find out where you fit into the model. If not, you can inexpensively buy books or online resources to give you a good idea of which personality style is most aligned with your communication and behavioral approaches.

## 360 Reviews

One of the best ways to learn about your blind spots, hidden strengths, and opportunities for improvement is a 360-degree feedback survey.

A 360 survey is one of the most valuable tools you can use to understand how others view you. Those great intentions you have and the results you get may translate into a less favorable perspective from employees than you expect.

You may recall from chapter 1 that it was a 360 review that painted a far different picture of how I viewed myself and how my colleagues viewed me. Although it was quite painful, it was exactly what I needed so that I could put a plan in place to start thinking differently.

A 360 review includes a self-evaluation and feedback from peers, direct reports, stakeholders, and others. Each rater responds anonymously to survey questions about your leadership competencies and provides responses to open-ended questions. Sometimes the individual being reviewed and the raters are interviewed by the person administering the survey as well.

The 360 review can be designed to include competencies you may be interested in learning about yourself. Examples of competencies include emotional intelligence (all areas), integrity and trust, communications, building teams, conflict management, strategic thinking, delegation, inclusivity, results, problem-solving, and resilience, to name a few.

If you work for a company that doesn't want to invest the time and money for a 360 review, you can develop your own using online forms and surveys. Invite team members, colleagues, and other relevant stakeholders to respond anonymously.

Ask your HR department if it's possible to schedule a 360 survey to gain insights into yourself. If that's not an option, you can create your own areas of competencies and questions using generative AI and ask someone to anonymously collect the feedback.

Or you can pose open-ended questions to your team, peers, or manager for feedback, such as: How can I run more effective meetings? What are your thoughts on how well I handled that situation? How could I have communicated our goals for the quarter more effectively? How clear was that training, and what could I do to improve? How would you rate the frequency and clarity of my communications, and what suggestions do you have for getting better at it?

The more specific questions you ask, the more valuable the answers are likely to be.

Remember, people mimic the leader. Asking for feedback and listening without defensiveness signals that you're humble, open, and committed to personal growth. And it also makes it easier for them to ask for and receive feedback from you.

## Leadership Coaching

Leadership coaching can be invaluable to those who want to continue improving and progressing in their career, just as elite athletes or musicians hire coaches to help them expand their potential and move to the next level.

A coach offers a fresh perspective and asks the kinds of questions to help you gain clarity on values, goals, and priorities. They can alert you to blind spots, assist in seeing things differently, and guide you in developing new habits and practices.

Hemant, one of my coaching clients, is a good example. One of his primary goals for coaching was to get control of his workday. He was working sixty hours a week and felt like his list of things to do was getting longer, not shorter.

He had delayed a large project for months and was getting pressure from his manager to complete it.

I asked, "What do you believe is causing you to delay this project?"

"I'm the only one who can do it, but I just can't find the bandwidth to put a lot of effort into it right now."

I continued, "Are your team members trained in the technology? Would this be a good growth opportunity for them?"

After a long pause, he said, "The answer is yes to both of those questions. I don't know why I didn't think of this. As a matter of fact, a couple of the guys have more training and experience than I do for this project."

A few months later, Hemant reported that the team had completed the project on schedule and within budget and had done it better than he would have.

Sometimes just a few simple questions can clear the noise or beliefs that hold you back.

You may be thinking that you can't afford a coach and that your company isn't going to pay for it. An alternative is to find someone within your company who you respect and ask them to meet with you once a month to be a thinking partner or mentor for you.

## Self-Reflection

I used to think that end-of-day reflection meant checking off items from my task list. Although it's a good way to measure progress, it's not a path to self-awareness. How *well* did you get things done? Did you leave any carnage behind? Let's look at a few things you may want to reflect on as well as questions to ask yourself.

**Emotional Recognition.** To reflect on emotions, ask yourself the following:

- Do I show up as the person I want to be? Describe how you do or don't.
- Can I identify specific triggers that cause strong emotional reactions (e.g., stress, frustration, excitement) when they occur?
- Do I notice when my mood is influencing the tone or direction of a conversation or meeting?
- When I'm upset, do I express my emotions constructively, or do I tend to react impulsively?

**Decision-Making.** You can reflect specifically on the decisions you made:

- Do I allow my emotions to cloud my judgment when making important decisions, or do I remain objective?
- When I need to make a difficult decision, do I take the time to process my emotions before acting?
- How often do I consider whether my emotions are influencing my strategic thinking or leadership effectiveness?
- Am I open to the ideas of others, or do I argue to be right?

**Stress and Resilience.** Consider these questions:

- How easily do I adapt my behavior when I realize my emotions are negatively influencing a situation?
- How do I handle stressful situations emotionally, and how does it affect my leadership approach?
- After experiencing emotional setbacks or challenges, how well do I bounce back?
- Do I blame others or make excuses for my shortcomings or unfavorable results?

Designating a time of day to reflect provides opportunities to identify recurring patterns or trends in behavior, thoughts, or reactions. Reflection is a great exercise for developing self-awareness. It can help you better understand your own emotions, which in turn makes it easier to recognize where changes may be needed.

## SELF-MANAGEMENT

Self-management is the step after developing awareness of triggers and emotions. It speaks to the choices you can make to manage your emotional reactions. It's not easy, because you're hardwired to experience emotion before your thinking brain kicks in, and yet it is possible to react to them in a thoughtful way.

In his book *Working with Emotional Intelligence*, Daniel Goleman relates the story of a multimillion-dollar emotional trigger. During a 1997 heavyweight boxing match, Evander Holyfield headbutted Mike Tyson, a repeat of something he'd done in a past match that Tyson lost. The second incident triggered Tyson's rage, and Holyfield's ear was in the wrong place at the wrong time—Tyson bit a chunk of it off! This lack of self-management cost Tyson a $3 million fine and a year's suspension from boxing (which probably cost him much more).[12]

Cortisol, the hormone released by our adrenal glands when stress kicks in, increases our heart rate and blood pressure to boost energy. Although the hormone might be useful in a stressful situation, it limits nonessential functions, such as the immune, digestive, and reproductive systems, and it reduces cognitive abilities. Cortisol stays in our system for several hours after being released. The constant flood of cortisol during high stress can cause anxiety, depression, digestive problems, headaches, muscle tension, heart disease, sleep problems, weight gain, and memory and concentration impairment.

Self-management starts by recognizing when we are emotionally triggered, becoming aware of our reaction, and taking the appropriate actions. For example, it's not helpful for a leader to raise their voice, demand that people work harder, or point out how a project behind schedule will reflect poorly to upper management. These actions add to the stress of all involved, including the recipients of the emotional reaction. Cortisol levels increase and cognitive capacity decreases. Lose-lose for everyone.

The good news is that humans, unlike other animals, can choose their reactions. Viktor Frankl, Austrian neurologist, psychologist, Holocaust survivor, and author, writes in his book *Man's Search for Meaning*, "Between stimulus and response, there is a space. In that space is our power to choose our response. In our response lies our growth and freedom."[13]

The space Frankl describes is the split second humans have to decide how to respond to a stimulus, such as what someone says or does to us. Will it be a knee-jerk reaction based on your emotions, or will you take the space for an intentional and appropriate response?

Fortunately, there are tactics to help develop self-management skills.

## TACTICS FOR IMPROVING SELF-MANAGEMENT

To improve self-management skills, it's critical to navigate the space between stimulus and response, making intentional choices that allow you to react in mindful ways. Here are several tactics that can help.

**Hit Pause.** Instead of an adverse reaction to a high-visibility project that is late, the response can be managed differently—by meeting with the team, asking questions, talking through the issues, getting a sense of their overwhelm, and exploring options to get help or asking for an exception to the due date. By alleviating the worry about a poor performance review or the stress of canceling weekend plans to work extra hours, cortisol levels go down and cognitive capacity increases.

When you experience an emotional trigger, time is your friend. How much time? That depends on the situation. A few deep breaths or counting to ten might give you the space to calm down and let your rational brain take over. Sometimes you might need an overnight or a few days to think things through. The key is to tamp down your amygdala response of fight, flight, or freeze and allow your reasoning brain (prefrontal cortex) time to process.

When I catch myself reacting emotionally and know I want to change my behavior, I'll ask for a redo. I stop and ask the person if we can start over, which helps me rewire my brain.

I ask the person to repeat what they said, and I'll take a deep breath before carefully choosing a more thoughtful response.

**Be Curious.** Curiosity also helps with self-management. Instead of an instinctive rejection of a perspective that's different from yours, ask for additional information: "That's interesting. Tell me more."

During a leadership workshop, Latasha was explaining her approach to solving a problem she had been dealing with. She had been speaking for no more than one minute when Logan, from another table, blurted, "That's not right!"

Tense energy quickly filled the room. People looked around, wondering how this would play out. I calmly asked Logan to let Latasha finish speaking. I turned to Latasha and said, "Please tell us more about your approach to the problem."

When she finished, I asked Logan if he had any questions or comments. He replied, "No. I should've let her finish. She's right."

After class, Logan waited for others to leave before he approached me. "I didn't realize how badly I came across in class with Latasha until you intervened. That was a helpful lesson. I need to listen more and talk less. I have a lot of work to do on that."

Practice building this mental muscle by asking one of your kids why they believe they should be allowed to stay out past midnight. Then suspend judgment and just listen. Remember that you can't use reasoning to change beliefs that are based on emotion. Be curious and practice listening.

**Be Proactive.** Sometimes you can anticipate a situation that may cause anxieties or stress and set boundaries in advance.

For example, if you are leading a meeting where one or two people tend to dominate the conversation, be explicit about expectations at the beginning. "We need to hear from each person in this meeting. Please limit your time to no more than three minutes. I will let you know when it's your turn."

**Stop Beating Yourself Up.** Most of us are overly critical of ourselves when we make a mistake. I know I am. Yet negative self-talk doesn't help. Instead of thinking, *I can't believe I made such a stupid mistake*, do a reframe. *Everyone makes mistakes, and I learned from it.* Recall Thomas Edison's famous quote when he was asked about failing ten thousand times before inventing the light bulb. "I have not failed. I've just found 10,000 ways that won't work." Don't dwell on the mistake or outcome.

**Regulate Your Voice Tone and Volume.** Raising your voice or speaking in an angry or sarcastic tone tends to escalate the situation. Pay attention to how you express yourself, including body language, tone, and words, to maintain calmness. If you're anticipating a difficult conversation, think ahead of time about how you will show up and how you will conduct yourself.

**Get Sufficient Sleep.** Cognitive abilities are greatly diminished when you are tired. Awareness and self-management take a lot of mental energy, and when you're sleep-deprived, the subconscious takes over and behaviors revert to autopilot. Mental breaks throughout the day will give your brain time to recharge.

Becoming self-aware and managing emotions and reactions in challenging situations isn't intuitive or second nature for most people. However, like most things, it becomes easier with practice and time. As a toddler learning to walk, you likely fell hundreds of times, but you kept at it until walking became habitual. Self-awareness and self-management take the same dedication.

## SOCIAL AWARENESS

Social awareness is the ability to shift from self-focus to understanding and empathizing with others' emotions. It involves recognizing social cues, interpreting body language, and being attuned to the emotional atmosphere in a group or an organization. Leaders who are strong in social awareness are empathetic and aware of and responsive to the needs of others, and they build better relationships.

Empathy is understanding and sharing the feelings of others. You put yourself in someone else's shoes and provide support that meets their emotional and practical needs. For example, one of your team members, Terry, is working on a high-priority report that is due later that day. He gets a call from day care that his daughter is running a fever of 102 degrees, and he needs to pick her up immediately. Chances are, you can relate to a situation like that. You tell Terry to take care of his daughter, and you'll take care of finishing the work or ask for an extension. Terry is relieved and can focus on the important thing, his daughter.

## TACTICS FOR IMPROVING SOCIAL AWARENESS

We can improve social awareness by implementing the following tactics.

**Listening and Body Language.** Active listening is a practice in which you listen carefully to discern another person's meaning without projecting your own thoughts onto them. If you're planning what to say next while someone else is talking, interrupting, finishing their sentence for them, or waiting impatiently for your turn to talk, you aren't listening at a level that helps you understand how the other person is feeling. Truly listening means focusing on another's emotions, not on yours.

Part of active listening also includes paying attention to facial expressions and body language. Crying, laughing, and anger are easy to recognize. But when emotions aren't as obvious, how do you tell what someone is feeling? Look at the person's body language, energy, and expressions. Are they smiling or frowning? Deep in thought? Perplexed? What is their posture? Arms crossed? Eye contact? Tone of voice? Do they seem engaged in the conversation, or are they less responsive?

If you're in a meeting and need to focus on participants' body language and facial expressions, ask someone else to take notes or record the meeting so that you can pay attention.

**Anticipate Emotions.** We've already established that our brain is hardwired to keep us in our comfort zone. Sometimes anticipating how a person might feel can pay huge dividends. For example, a new employee is excited about a job, but working in a new environment with new people, a different culture, and unknown team dynamics can create anxiety. To demonstrate social awareness, you can welcome new hires before they start, introduce them to the team, and answer questions they might have.

Change also often causes stress, especially if it is a big change like being acquired by another company or implementing new systems and processes. Plan to spend more time—a *lot* more time than you think is needed—overcommunicating. It's hard to provide too much reassurance if someone is worried about losing their job.

Some changes may include a difficult personal situation, such as the loss of a parent or close friend, a divorce, or an unexpected diagnosis. Meet with the individual privately to see if they want to share what's bothering them. Although you don't want to pry into someone's personal life or make them feel uncomfortable, you can let them know you noticed a change and are willing to listen in confidence. Some people are private and prefer not to talk, but you still can let them know you care about their well-being. Keep the information confidential—it's not yours to share.

Social awareness skills are not always easy or intuitive, especially for those of us who are task-focused first and people-focused second. Your social awareness skills are important in your leadership role. Relationships with your team members are stronger when you show empathy and understanding. You create a more inclusive and emotionally safe work environment. Your team members feel seen, heard, and valued, which leads to higher engagement, morale, and productivity.

## RELATIONSHIP MANAGEMENT

This last component of EI is the ability to build, maintain, and nurture productive and positive relationships, manage conflict effectively, and inspire collaboration. It requires mastering self-awareness, self-management, and social awareness to build meaningful relationships. Your ability to successfully manage interactions with others plays an important role in leading people.

Conflicts arise on a regular basis, and it's your job to resolve them professionally. This is much easier when you have built relationships and when people trust you to do the right thing.

Let me give you a personal example. I was the program manager for a large contract with a federal government agency. The government contracting officer, Margaret, had a reputation for being difficult to work with. She was known for terminating contracts for default if she didn't think the government contractor was doing a good job. My predecessor had been removed from the role, and I was asked to be his replacement.

After the change was announced, I scheduled a meeting with Margaret. When I went to her office, I noticed a bullwhip hanging over a clock on the wall. Then I saw a woman with a stern look sitting behind a large wooden desk. She had not been happy with the prior program manager and had several concerns about performance.

After introductions, I started the conversation by saying, "Interesting office decor," then nodding toward the bullwhip.

She replied, "A contractor gave me that."

"Margaret, I'm not smart enough to be manipulative or to lie. I'm here to do the best job on your contract that I can. Our team won't always do everything perfectly. However, I promise that you will be the second person, after myself, to know if something is going sideways. I will always tell you the truth, and I would like the same from you. I know we have issues to resolve, and I'll commit to you that we will deal with each one quickly. Would you tell me the things that cause you the most stress and frustration?"

She seemed a little taken aback and then started to smile. "You and I will get along just fine. I don't like being blindsided by missed schedules, especially on high-priority programs with high visibility. I expect people to do what they say they will do."

Margaret and I met regularly to discuss status, issues, and

concerns. When we had bimonthly contract meetings with a larger group from both teams, we had already decided how to handle issues. Project negotiations were cordial, and we both strived for a win-win outcome. We worked together well for the two years I managed the contract.

When I left my company for another opportunity, she was there for my going-away party—the first time she had attended a government contractor event. We developed a tremendous amount of respect for each other during our tenure together and kept in touch for years.

Interestingly, within a year of my departure from the contract, Margaret issued a termination for default to my prior company. My replacement opted not to heed my advice on building a strong relationship with her and wanted to do things her way.

Never underestimate the importance of building meaningful relationships.

## TACTICS FOR IMPROVING RELATIONSHIP MANAGEMENT

Most of the tactics described earlier in this chapter apply to relationship management and aren't repeated. Let's look at a few ways to be intentional about improving this EI component.

**Relationship Inventory.** Develop a list of people with whom you need or want to develop professional relationships, such as your team members, manager, peers, colleagues, and other stakeholders (internal and external). The one-on-one meeting with individual team members is an optimal way to learn about them and their needs and desires and to share things about your leadership style, personal interests, and so on.

You can also use the one-on-one meeting with your manager and in other interactions to build a relationship with them. What if your manager is too busy? Try to get on their calendar, maybe for lunch or breakfast before work. Be explicit about what you want to accomplish with them (e.g., understand what problems they are facing and how you can help, their opinion of what it takes to be successful in your role, and what their hot buttons are). You won't come across as a stalker when you are intentional about objectives.

Reach out to peers, colleagues, and stakeholders to ask for fifteen minutes of their time to introduce yourself and learn about their roles and how you and your team work with them and to possibly solicit feedback.

Prepare a list of questions to help you learn more about them. Look at their social media platforms to determine their interests if you don't know anything about them. Think about what you want to share about yourself (and the team). When you meet, smile, speak clearly, and make eye contact. If you're asked a question that you don't know the answer to, make a note and let them know when you'll get back to them. Then follow up when you said you would.

On your calendar, set reminders to check in periodically to continue building the relationship. If you happen to see an article or event that may be of interest, send it to them. Look for ways to add value to them.

**The Long Haul.** Relationship-building isn't a one-and-done event—it's ongoing. Invest in the development of team members. Make the one-on-one meetings important and meaningful. Use your social awareness skills to understand how others are feeling and show empathy.

Stay connected to past colleagues and continue to offer value, even when roles change. Invest in your relationships to create goodwill and support that can be used when needed.

Our home and work lives are fraught with stressful situations, conflicts, and challenges. Strong relationships and trust go a long way toward defusing tensions and promoting safe working environments.

## EMOTIONAL INTELLIGENCE IN PRACTICE

We've covered definitions of each of the four EI components. How do high and low EI look in the workplace? Let's take two people at the director level of a company, Marilyn and Mason, and look at their interactions at work.

In a morning meeting, the CEO announces that their company has been acquired by a larger corporation. She assures the leadership team that the acquisition is for the best and will bring new opportunities. It also would likely bring rumors and uncertainty about potential layoffs and culture change.

The acquiring company would be announcing the acquisition at their quarterly shareholders' meeting the next day. Marilyn and Mason are among leaders in the company asked to communicate the news to their teams that afternoon. They are given high-level talking points to guide the conversation.

Marilyn gathers her team, takes a deep breath, and begins with a calm, empathetic tone. "I have important news to share with you all. Our company has been acquired by a large organization. I know this is unexpected and might bring up a lot of emotions, and that's OK. I want to create a space where we can talk about this as a team." She pauses to let the words sink in, carefully observing the reactions of her team.

"This transition over the next few months could bring

exciting opportunities, but I understand there may be concerns. I don't have all the details yet, but I promise to be transparent as I learn more."

One employee asks, "What does this mean for our jobs? Will there be layoffs?"

"That's a great question. Right now, I don't have any information about specific changes, but I'll do everything in my power to advocate for this team. My goal is to make sure that we are in the best possible position moving forward."

Another team member asks, "What will happen to our culture?"

"That's another important concern," Marilyn replies. "This team has built something really special, and I'm committed to preserving as much of that as possible. I'd love to hear your ideas on how we can carry our culture forward during this transition."

Over the next several days, Marilyn follows up with individual team members to see how they're processing the news. Several are concerned about potential layoffs. Marilyn listens carefully and offers reassurance. "Change is hard, and it's OK to feel worried," she says. "Let's focus on what we can control right now. I'm here to support you."

Mason gathers his team and comes into the conference room with a clipboard and a neutral expression. He launches into his announcement. "All right, team. Here's what's happening. Our company has been acquired. This is a done deal, and it's going to mean some changes around here. That's business. Let's not overthink it." He scans the room quickly but doesn't pause to gauge the reactions of his team members.

"From what I've been told, this will bring opportunities for growth, but we'll also need to adapt to the way the new parent company operates. I don't have all the details yet, so there's no point in speculating. Just stay focused on your work."

One employee cautiously raises his hand. "Do you know if this means layoffs?"

Mason sighs. "I don't know. I may lose my job. When I know, you'll know. For now, let's not waste time worrying about what might happen. Focus on what's in front of you. That's what I'm going to do."

Another employee asks, "What about our team culture? Will it change?"

Mason shrugs. "Probably. Look, things like culture evolve over time. We'll figure it out as we go."

After the meeting, Mason retreats to his office, believing that he has efficiently delivered the message. He avoids further discussions, seeing questions as distractions from real work. Over the next several days, tensions grow within his team. When some attempt to approach Mason for clarity, he gives dismissive responses—"Let's not get emotional about this" or "Just keep doing your job." Frustration continues to increase.

Marilyn's team felt valued and heard. They were motivated even with the uncertainty. Mason's team, on the other hand, was demoralized and started to disengage. Mason blames the dip in performance on people overreacting rather than on his leadership approach.

Marilyn's high EI allowed her to handle the announcement with empathy, transparency, and a focus on building trust. She addressed her team's emotions and concerns head-on, creating a sense of control amid the uncertainty.

Mason's low EI led to a lack of connection, dismissive communication, and a missed opportunity to support his team during an emotionally challenging time. His inability to empathize with their concerns created fear and disengagement.

The importance of emotional intelligence can't be overemphasized. As research has shown, it's the difference between leadership success or failure. Higher EI helps you build trust with your team members and with others. It also directly affects the people you lead, both at work and at home. When an employee leaves work feeling seen, heard, and valued, they are less likely to carry workplace stress home to their families. Less stress means better relationships and improved health.

## EMOTIONAL INTELLIGENCE IS A JOURNEY

If you're thinking that developing high EI takes soul-searching, self-reflection, overcoming years of limiting beliefs and habits, and is a lot of work, you're right. The good news is that you don't need to do it all at once. Success isn't about being the best—it's about being better today than you were yesterday. Choose one or two things to work on. For example, you could practice active listening skills in a meeting or by reading a room and looking for reactions that you may otherwise miss. Ask a trusted colleague or friend to provide feedback on perceived blind spots and develop a plan to overcome them. When a setback occurs, reframe the challenge in a way that helps you learn. Take an EI assessment to see where you excel and where you may have potential areas for improvement.

Maybe you're thinking, *I've been promoted several times, so I must be doing things right.* You probably are doing a lot of things right. Keep doing those things. Maybe you're like me, where I was promoted because of getting results. That only went so far before my lack of EI caught up to me. My career would likely have been much different had I known about the importance of the people side early on. I missed a lot of opportunities to positively influence others.

You've been given assessments and suggestions for how to identify strengths and areas that need attention. We're all human, which means we aren't perfect. For most people, developing high emotional intelligence is a lifelong journey. It certainly is for me.

Awareness

High-Performing Teams

Lead by Example

Effective Communication

Exceptional Results

Productivity Habits

# PART THREE

## EFFECTIVE COMMUNICATION

The single biggest problem in communication
is the illusion that it has taken place.

**—GEORGE BERNARD SHAW**

**EFFECTIVE COMMUNICATION IS TOUTED** as one of the most important skills a leader can possess, but it has never been more challenging. For the first time in history, today's workforce spans four generations—baby boomers, Generation X, millennials, and Generation Z—each with their own communication styles and preferences. Older generations may prefer face-to-face communication or a phone call. Younger employees tend to be more comfortable with email, texting, and chat messages—and expect quick responses. This makes effective communication, never easy to begin with, a monumental challenge.

The shift to remote and hybrid work has added further complexity. Reading body language is impossible on a phone call and challenging in video meetings. Without tone and body language, texts and chat messages can be interpreted in unintended ways. Informal office interactions where relationships are often built have diminished.

Globalization, with multiple time zones, cultural differences, and communication styles, also exacerbates communication challenges. What is considered common and acceptable in one country may be offensive in other cultures.

Communication is rightly regarded as among the most critical and essential skills for effective leaders. It's foundational for conveying vision, aligning teams, resolving conflicts, and getting results.

The first skill to master for effective communication is the ability to actively listen.

# CHAPTER SEVEN

# ACTIVE LISTENING

**VINCE, A COLLEAGUE I HAD WORKED** with several years ago, sent me an email asking if we could talk. He had worked his way up in his twelve-year tenure in his company, from project manager to senior director, with multiple teams reporting to him. Attached to the email was a file with a 360 feedback report.

When we met, Vince told me that he had always prided himself on being a good communicator. "I have an open-door policy, weekly team meetings, and communicate information with regular emails. When I got the report I sent you, I was expecting to see feedback on how well I communicate. Instead, I got comments like 'Vince often interrupts during meetings, making it hard for others to express their ideas,' and 'Vince tends to dominate conversations, and it feels like he's already made up his mind before hearing others out,' and, from my manager, 'Vince is great at presenting ideas, but there's a noticeable gap when it comes to listening. He could benefit from pausing more and engaging others in deeper conversations.'"

Vince was surprised by this feedback. During our conversation, he interrupted me a couple of times before I finished my point. While I was talking, I could see his wheels turning and knew that he wasn't really paying attention to what I was saying. When I pointed this out, he started to understand the relevance of the comments.

I suggested that he schedule one-on-one meetings with his direct reports, several of his peers, and his manager to ask for feedback on how he could improve his communication skills. A few months later, Vince and I had a much different conversation. "I didn't realize how much information I was missing until I really started listening. I also didn't realize how much I frustrated my team members and caused them to shut down. There's a noticeable difference in how much better we all communicate now that I've learned how to listen and hear what others are saying." Like most things, active listening is a skill that can be developed using tactics.

Most of us assume that we are good listeners, but are we really? How often do you start thinking about something else when another person is talking? Or have to replay a portion of an audiobook because your mind drifted to other thoughts?

One of the keys to mastering communication skills is not just learning how to deliver a message; it's also about listening, being open to diverse viewpoints, and adapting communication methods to different personality styles and audiences, as discussed earlier. Leo Rosten, American writer and humorist, said, "Why did God give me two ears and one mouth? So I would talk less and listen more." Author Stephen Covey highlights the problem more directly: "Most people do not listen with the intent to understand; they listen with the intent to reply." Some people are so eager to reply (or argue to prove they are right) that they cut off the person speaking and blurt their response.

When it comes to communications, the importance of listening is often overlooked, yet it's the secret ingredient when interacting with others.

## THE BENEFITS OF
## AN ACTIVE LISTENING CULTURE

Being a good listener pays more dividends than connecting and building trust with individuals. It also demonstrates respect to others and creates an environment where people feel valued and appreciated. This in turn fosters a culture in which people feel safe and are more engaged in their work, as previously discussed in chapter 3.

Creating a listening culture sets the tone for team dynamics. You know that people mimic the leader. By actively listening, you set an example for the rest of the team. When your employees see that you're engaged, empathetic, and focused during conversations, they are more likely to model that behavior in their interactions with colleagues, clients, and other stakeholders.

Active listening helps you hear the whole message, which means specific details are presented that may uncover problem areas or new ideas. The likelihood of missing critical pieces of information is prevented or minimized when the bigger picture is understood.

An active listening culture improves problem-solving and decision-making in several ways. Team members are more likely to share their perspectives and ideas, providing solutions and viewpoints that may not have been considered otherwise.

The risk of miscommunicating or misunderstanding is reduced when everyone is listening to understand the problem or decision to be made. The result is better solutions and more informed decisions that are more suited to the team's needs and priorities.

Active listening also helps break down silos among other departments and teams. It's important to understand where you and your team fit into the bigger picture. How can you contribute to other areas in the company? When you encourage cross-functional communications and value input from people outside your team, it's possible to create a more integrated and collaborative culture where information flows more freely.

## OVERCOMING BARRIERS TO ACTIVE LISTENING

Some people are better at actively listening than others. For example, people who are naturally observant pay close attention not only to what's being said but also to what isn't being said. They notice subtle changes in voice tone and body language, which helps them gain a better understanding of the speaker's message. People-centered individuals are naturally focused on the well-being of others and are excellent listeners because they prioritize relationships over tasks. People who are naturally calm don't often let their emotions take over during conversations, which helps them stay focused on the speaker and respond in a thoughtful, measured way.

Then there's the rest of us. If you're like me, active listening is not a natural tendency. Let's look at some of the challenges leaders and others must deal with to engage in active listening. The following section provides tactics to help improve in each of these areas.

**Distractions.** Workplace distractions are rampant, from notifications on your cell phone and smartwatch to calendar reminders, impromptu interruptions, chat dings, and incoming emails. Internal distractions like looming deadlines, a prior meeting that didn't go well, or an upcoming difficult conversation are hard to compartmentalize. If you're working remotely, household distractions like delivery people, dogs barking, or a family member wanting your attention also come into play. With all the external and internal noise, you may miss key points or fail to pick up on important emotional cues that are needed to fully understand the message your team member wants to impart to you.

Tactics to minimize external distractions include the following:

- Set your phone to silent or put it in airplane mode. Turn off email, messaging, chat, social media, and any other application notifications. This helps you avoid the temptation of glancing at your phone or being pulled away by unnecessary alerts, which derail your ability to concentrate on the conversation at hand.

- Use the do-not-disturb features on your phone and computer to ensure that no external interruptions shift your focus.

- Close any unnecessary applications or windows to resist the urge to multitask.

- For in-person meetings, find a location that is conducive to active listening, like a quiet conference room. Place your phone face down, or better, out of sight.

External distractions are more easily addressed by simply removing them or turning them off. Internal distractions, however, require a different approach. Stress, anxiety, or preoccupation with other tasks can pull your focus away from the person speaking. Tactics for being more mindful include the following:

- Take a few deep breaths before entering the conversation and center your focus. This helps reduce internal chatter and allows you to be calmer and more present.

- Focus on the speaker's voice and the words they are saying. Redirect your attention if you find your mind wandering. This is especially useful in virtual meetings where external distractions may be out of your control.

- Pay attention to your own body language. Are you fidgeting? Is your posture open and receptive, or are your arms crossed? Is your facial expression intense?

Another tactic you can use to help focus is to set a pre-meeting routine. Prepare key questions or thoughts to help you focus on what's important. You may also want to clear your desk if the meeting is happening in your office. For virtual meetings, close all unneeded windows and tabs. These actions help you stay present during the conversation.

These tactics for minimizing external and internal distractions will help you become more present in the current moment by enabling your ability to focus.

**Mental Responses.** We think faster than we speak. The average person speaks at about 135 to 175 words per minute but can listen to 400 to 500 words per minute. The difference between the speaker's talking speed and the much faster listening speed provides sufficient time for the listener to tune in and out, think about what they are going to say, or drift off. As author Stephen Covey points out in *The 7 Habits of Highly Effective People*, most people are thinking about their response while the other person is still talking.[1] This tendency leads to disengagement from the conversation and makes it impossible to truly hear what is being said. In virtual situations, this is even worse because it's easier to think about something else during virtual conversations, drifting in and out of the discussion.

Several tactics can help you focus on the conversation instead of on your response:

- Practice paraphrasing what has been said after a key point, not just repeating what was said. For example, "So what I am hearing is . . ." or "It sounds like you're saying . . ."

- Ask clarifying questions. For instance, "Can you explain more about what you meant by that?" or "What led you to that conclusion?" When you're curious about what is being said, it can improve how you listen.

- Avoid jumping to conclusions or solutions. As a leader, you may already know what advice to give, but doing so too quickly can interrupt the flow of the conversation and prevent you from fully understanding the situation.

- Practice empathetic listening. Pick up on the speaker's emotion, tone, and underlying feelings behind the words. For example, if you're in a meeting with a team member who is venting about a heavy workload, you want to make eye contact, nod to reassure the person that you're understanding them, and maintain an open posture. You can paraphrase and reflect their feelings by saying, "It sounds like you're feeling overwhelmed with the amount of work on your plate. I can see how that would be stressful, especially with all the deadlines coming up. Let's take a look at your workload and see what we can adjust to make it more manageable."

These tactics can help you overcome the urge to respond too quickly or cut someone off while they are speaking.

**Time Pressures.** If you're like most leaders, time may feel like a scarce resource. You have much more work to do than the time allotted to do it. Each meeting or conversation can seem like time that takes away from the "real" work. If you allow time pressures to affect your listening skills, it may cause misunderstandings, reduced trust, and missed opportunities for meaningful communication and connection.

Marcus, the CTO of a multibillion-dollar company, has been a client for years. His calendar is crammed with meetings and travel, but his busy schedule doesn't affect his ability to actively listen. When we meet, whether in person or on a video call, he gives me his undivided attention. He makes me feel like I'm the only person who matters at that time. He most always has more important things to deal with than a call with me, but I'd never know it. He's mastered active listening.

The following are a few tactics to help you manage your time pressures while practicing active listening skills:

- Reframe how you view active listening from a passive task to a strategic leadership skill. Treat listening with the same level of importance as other high-priority tasks. Because it *is*. It's hard to build trust and connect with your team members and others if you don't fully listen and understand what is being communicated.

- Center yourself by taking a few deep breaths to reset your focus. Remind yourself that rushing through the conversation won't lead to the best outcome and that being present will actually save time in the long run.

- Set clear expectations for how much time you have for a conversation. For example, you can say, "I have set aside thirty minutes to discuss this issue and have a hard stop. Let's focus on the most important areas first. We can schedule a follow-on meeting to discuss solutions." Then you can remind the other person when you have five minutes left.

- Acknowledge your time pressures up front. For instance, "I understand we have a lot to cover, and I want to make sure we use our time wisely. Let's focus on the key issues first. If we need more time, we'll schedule another meeting to continue our discussion."

- Don't rush the end of the meeting. Acknowledge that the conversation is valuable and reassure the other person that it will be continued as needed. You can also ask the person to send additional thoughts or details through email so that nothing is missed. For example, "Feel free to send me an email with any additional points, and I'll review them before our next meeting. This will help us move through them more quickly."

Active listening doesn't have to be time-consuming—it's about quality, not quantity. When you make listening a priority, despite time pressures, you demonstrate respect, build trust, and encourage more meaningful and productive conversations with team members and others.

**Prejudgments and Assumptions.** Most of us enter conversations with our own set of beliefs and assumptions that can cloud our ability to listen closely to what someone is saying. We may also believe that we already know what someone will say and stop listening.

Remember that our RAS filters out things that don't align with our beliefs, making it more likely to limit our ability to hear the actual message. These mental shortcuts can lead to miscommunication and strained relationships. The dialogue between Logan and Latasha in chapter 6 was a clear example of this. Logan was convinced that he knew what Latasha was saying and cut her off to tell her she was wrong in her thinking. After giving her a chance to continue her explanation, he agreed with her solution.

Let's look at tactics you can use to be more open-minded and to suspend assumptions:

- Challenge any assumptions you may be making by asking yourself questions like these: Am I assuming something about this person or situation that may not be true? What if I'm wrong? Do I have biases around this topic or toward this person?

- Rather than relying on assumptions, look for specific evidence to support or refute your thoughts. For example, instead of assuming that someone is upset based on their voice tone, ask, "What's on your mind?" Respond to facts, not assumptions.

- Be curious instead of assuming that you already know the other person's thoughts or intentions. Ask yourself, *What can I learn from this person right now?* Accept that you may not have all the answers and may not understand the other person's perspective initially.

- Ask for more information so that the team member can explain their thoughts in more detail. For example, "What's the main challenge you're facing right now?" This helps you uncover underlying thoughts or emotions that aren't apparent.

- Ask the person you're talking with to clarify anything that is unclear or contradictory to your assumptions. For example, "Earlier I thought you said that the project timeline was manageable—has something changed?" When I hear someone use the phrase "They said . . ." or "Everyone thinks . . .," I ask for clarification about *they* and *everyone*. This generalization may turn out to be just one person's opinion.

I find that actively listening in conversations doesn't leave any time for my mind to wander. I'm genuinely interested in what the other person is saying and am engaged in the conversation, paraphrasing and asking questions for clarity.

I love this quote from Maya Angelou: "People will forget what you said. People will forget what you did. But people will never forget how you made them feel."

# CHAPTER EIGHT

# THE NEED FOR CLARITY

**EARLIER IN MY CAREER,** one of my employees put a copy of a document on my desk with a note that read, "Would you review this, please?" With red pen in hand, I spent a couple of hours going through it carefully, making grammar changes, writing comments and questions in the margins, and rewriting parts of it. I put the marked-up copy on the employee's desk and left for the evening. The next morning, the employee came in, handed me a new red ink pen, and said, "Based on your markups, I'm pretty sure that you'll be needing a new pen soon. I only wanted you to review the document to see if it was in the right format. It was just a very rough draft."

How many times has this happened to you? Maybe you've not been as clear as you should have been, realizing after the fact that someone spent time working on the wrong thing.

## CLEAR COMMUNICATIONS

In *The Power of Clarity*, author Ann Latham writes, "As much as 80 percent of employee time is lost to confusion and counterproductive activities."[2]

Latham helps us understand her perspective by describing

two types of verbs. The first type is called a treadmill verb that has no clear purpose and can result in confusion and miscommunications. Examples of treadmill verbs include the following: review, provide feedback, report, inform, discuss, check in, follow up, and look into this. It's easy to see how these verbs can create confusion. What exactly should I be reviewing? Format, content, visual presentation, fitness for audience? Or what am I following up on? Status, financials, staffing? We see treadmill verbs used almost every day without clarification.

The second category is destination verbs. These are verbs that demand an outcome. Examples include decide (decision), plan (plan of action to know what to do by when), resolve (resolution), list (list to know when done), confirm (confirmation), authorize (authorization), question (list of questions), and answer (list of alternatives).

The goal is to turn ambiguous verbs into ones with clarity and actionable outcomes. In my opening red pen example, it would've saved me a lot of time if the request had been phrased as "Please let me know if you approve the document format" instead of as "Please review." The clarifying request would have taken only a few minutes.

When you see yourself putting "Please review" in an email subject line or when sharing a document, take the next steps and be specific about what you are asking for. Do you want a review of content appropriateness, accuracy, and completeness? If so, a better request is this: "Please confirm that the content is appropriate, accurate, and complete. If you see anything missing or that needs correction, please list at the bottom of the document." Also include the date by which you need the information from the reviewer.

Are you asking a reviewer for approval to move forward with implementing what a document includes? If so, be specific in your ask: "Please authorize the team to move forward with the plan in the document" versus "Please review and let me know if you think this is OK."

Project updates are fraught with confusion. What, exactly, does "project update" mean? Be explicit. Do you have a project plan? Is the project on schedule? On budget? Do you have the needed team resources? Are stakeholders providing necessary information? What are the key risks and issues? How are these being mitigated? What assistance do you need from me? Otherwise, people spend time talking about things they got done but don't provide information that leads to action. Use a project status template to capture the clarity needed with instructions on the key areas of interest.

Checklists and templates are great ways to know what is needed and when the work is complete. They also increase productivity because the steps are clearly outlined and provide consistency in how the work is done.

"Please provide your feedback" on a document can mean a lot of things. For example, perhaps what you really want is a decision or confirmation on something. "We can go in one of two directions. Here are the pros and cons of each. The team recommends this approach. Please confirm our recommendation by noon tomorrow."

It's easy to see how treadmill verbs create confusion, rework, and frustrations. As the leader, you may get requests from your manager to "please review," "check into this," or "give us an update." You immediately recognize the ambiguity in the requests and know the right thing to do is to ask clarifying questions.

You may be thinking, *If I ask questions, my boss will think I don't know what I'm doing. Perhaps I should make a best guess at what is needed and take my chances.* Maybe, but you could also use this as an opportunity to build your credibility. Instead of asking something like "What do you mean by 'review'?" you could say, "I'd like to make sure that I provide what you're looking for on this assignment. What outcomes would you like me to bring as a result of this review? Is there any part of the assignment I should focus on first that would be beneficial to you? Is there a particular format you'd like to see? I want to make sure I meet your expectations."

If you are uncertain about a request or a situation, ask questions in a mindful way that shows your desire to do good work.

## FRAMING CONVERSATIONS

How many times have you been in a meeting or someone starts a conversation and you had to play the fifty questions game to figure out what was being discussed? Sometimes it seems like others expect us to read their minds and magically know what they are talking about or what they need. We don't understand the context, they're using acronyms we've never heard of, and we aren't sure if they need help or just need to vent. This can be frustrating, waste our time, and lead to misunderstandings. Let's look at framing to help improve communications.

In leadership, *how* you communicate is just as important as *what* you communicate. Framing the conversation is one of your most important tools for effective communication. Framing sets the tone, context, and expectations for the discussion, ensuring that everyone is on the same page. When done well, it can prevent misunderstandings, reduce tension, and lead to a more successful exchange.

What follows are a few tips to help you frame conversations.

**Start with the Purpose and Desired Outcome.** Before you begin an important conversation, define why you're having it. What do you hope to accomplish? For example, "I'd like to have a quick conversation about the issues on the project timelines and decide how best to stay on track. Let's meet today at three." You and your team are clear on why you're meeting, and the desired outcome is a decision for getting the project on track.

**Provide Context.** Not all communications are as straightforward as the last example. Sometimes you need to provide background information for others to understand the bigger picture and why it's important. For example, "I need to provide a brief overview of the analysis that was done to help clarify the alternative solutions."

**Set Time Boundaries.** Sometimes you have someone who likes to talk, and conciseness is not one of their strengths. And sometimes you need to protect your time. Tell the other person how much time you have for the conversation. "I have a hard stop in thirty minutes. Let's cover the most important points and identify next steps." This tends to help keep people focused and minimize tangents.

**Elicit Participation.** In conversations where you want collaboration from everyone, let the group know. "I'd really appreciate hearing everyone's thoughts on this issue. I want us to collaborate and come up with the best solution together."

Participants are put on notice that they need to bring their ideas to the table.

**Anticipate Emotions.** As a leader, you will likely have many conversations that could escalate emotions or defensiveness. To help defuse the situation, frame the discussion in a neutral and objective way, focusing on facts, not blame, and suggest solving the problem together. "We've noticed some challenges in communications between departments. Instead of pointing fingers, let's figure out how we can improve the process going forward."

**Close with a Summary.** Once the conversation is ending, summarize the main points, outline any next steps, and assign responsibilities. This helps everyone leave with clarity on what was discussed and what needs to happen next. "To recap, we've agreed on three actions to resolve the schedule delay. I'll send out an email outlining the steps and schedule a meeting next Monday to check on progress."

Properly framing conversations helps you manage expectations, reduce misunderstandings, and ensure a more meaningful dialogue. This in turn creates a team culture built on trust, clarity, and effective communication.

## COMMUNICATING CLEAR EXPECTATIONS

Everyone deserves to have clear expectations from the leader, from the team members to other departments.

It makes sense that when we use our GPS on a road trip, we arrive sooner and in a better mood than if we guessed our way there, stopping along the way to ask for directions from people we hope can help us. The same is true with our work.

Donald Miller, author and sales and marketing expert, says, "No one wants to live a mystery every day wondering what they are supposed to do."

Don't assume that your team can read your mind. Be explicit in what you expect up front so that there is no ambiguity. What may be common sense to you is anything but common for someone else. It's much easier to set expectations early on than to have uncomfortable conversations later. Expectation setting/clarification is not a one-and-done thing; it requires ongoing attention and revisions.

Let's look at ways you can set behavioral and performance expectations for team members. Behavioral expectations are those related to professional conduct, ethics, respect, interpersonal interactions, and communications. I have found it helpful to document these and communicate them formally so that there can be no excuses that someone didn't know they were supposed to play nicely with others and do their work.

Common behavioral team expectations to consider include the following:

- Be respectful to others.
- Be willing to help out in other areas versus saying, "It's not my job."
- Be willing to invest in yourself. Learn new things and teach others.
- Ask for help when you don't know or can't find the answer.
- Keep a positive attitude and be encouraging to others.
- Don't participate in or start rumors.
- Be open to feedback without being defensive.
- Hold yourself accountable for your work, completing

assignments on time or providing advance notice when something may be late.

- Be on time for meetings and come prepared.
- Take initiative and don't wait to be told what to do.
- Be flexible with work assignments, knowing that things may change from time to time.
- No surprises—communicate needed information, the good and the bad.

During the pandemic, I found it helpful (necessary) to be explicit about expectations for video meetings, especially for those who weren't accustomed to remote work.

- Turn on cameras for appropriate meetings; specify video-free days.
- Do not wear pajamas or sweaty exercise tank tops or use exercise equipment when on a video call. Dress appropriately and be still.
- Practice active listening. No checking chats, emails, or texts during video calls.
- Don't have side chats during the call. Stay focused; we all know what you're doing.
- Mute your audio when not speaking to minimize background noise.
- Minimize background distractions.
- Give everyone a chance to contribute to the conversation.
- Raise the virtual hand instead of talking over someone.

Performance expectations are needed to outline what is expected from employees related to their job duties and responsibilities. They set the standard for evaluating and measuring team performance. Performance expectations are essential for providing clarity and aligning employee efforts. These also provide the basis for providing feedback and input into an employee's performance review.

Many different types of job roles exist, each with its own unique set of performance expectations, with some easier to identify than others. Roles that follow established workflows and processes are more quantitative in nature and are easier to determine. For example, a mortgage underwriter knows how many loans are expected to be underwritten on a daily or weekly basis, call center associates know how many resolved calls are expected each day, recruiters know the expected number of monthly hires, and team leaders are measured on team productivity and quality—you get the idea.

Other roles may not be quite as clear-cut. For a manager role, expectations may include measures such as these:

- Have regularly scheduled one-on-one meetings with all team members.
- Lead <number of> book studies for your team annually/<number of> training classes.
- Maintain an average employee engagement score of <percentage engaged>. (Note: This can be measured using employee engagement surveys.)
- Complete <list of projects> within <time frame>.
- Achieve customer satisfaction rating of <percentage>.

Performance measures should be based on outcomes, not on tasks. This encourages accountability and autonomy and leads to a sense of purpose. Knowledge workers, in particular, want an autonomous working environment to be creative and not limited to set ways of doing things. This leads to new avenues of thinking and innovation.

Let's take the example of setting expectations for a project manager. You've been asked to lead one of the larger cross-functional projects in the company. You've been assigned a project manager, Eric, who recently joined the project management office and who appears to have the requisite skills and experience for the project. Even though you have confidence in Eric based on his credentials, it's still a worthwhile exercise to meet with him to review your expectations.

The conversation may go something like this: "I'm happy to have you assigned to this project and have every confidence that you'll be able to deliver. To make sure we're on the same page, I'd like to go over what I need from you in your role.

"First and foremost, this is a high-priority project with monthly senior management briefings. There can't be any surprises. If you think something is going off the rails, I want to know as soon as you know. My cell phone is the best way to reach me quickly.

"Second, as part of a weekly thirty-minute status meeting, I want to know if we're on schedule and within budget as well as key risks and issues with mitigation strategies and where you need help.

"I'm interested in knowing when each key milestone is due and when we hit it so that we can celebrate the success and provide recognition to those who went above and beyond to get it done. Let's be sure to recognize teams and individuals who are making the biggest impact and contributions. We want to monitor the workload to keep team morale high.

"Regarding project meetings—please be sure you provide an agenda with any upfront work distributed at least forty-eight hours in advance to give participants time to review. If you are invited to meetings without agendas, please ask for clarification.

"We need our schedule to be realistic, not set up as a death march. Working overtime should be reserved only when we need to catch up. If anyone gets pulled off the project, if you can't get the needed resources, or if anything else happens that affects the schedule, please let me know quickly. I'm here to help you and remove roadblocks that are slowing you down."

This conversation lets the project manager know what your leadership style is and your expectations. As vulnerability expert and author Brené Brown says, "Clear is kind; unclear is unkind."

We've covered the importance of words to use for clarity, establishing the context of conversations using framing, and setting clear expectations. Let's look at a few tools you can employ to become an effective communicator.

## THE PERSONAL OPERATING GUIDE

One of my favorite tools is the personal operating guide, a template to help you and your team better understand how each person prefers to work and communicate. Earlier, I introduced the DiSC personality questionnaire. The personal operating guide takes it a step further and provides additional insights.

What follows is a sample guide for you to use as is or tailor to your needs. Consider implementing it as an engaging exercise during team meetings, where each person shares their information. Make it fun!

| CATEGORY | DESCRIPTION/EXAMPLES |
|---|---|
| Communication Style | **Preferred:** Email, face-to-face/video for important topics<br>**Best time:** After lunch<br>**Do:** Be direct and concise<br>**Don't:** Send long emails |
| Recognition | **Preferred:** Private thanks or in team meeting |
| Feedback | **Preferred:** One-on-one meeting, constructive and solution-focused<br>**Do:** Offer suggestions<br>**Don't:** Delay feedback or criticize in public |
| Likes | **Preferences:** Collaboration, clear goals<br>**Environment:** Mix of autonomy and team collaboration |
| Dislikes | **Pet peeves:** Last-minute changes, lack of transparency<br>**Avoid:** Micromanagement, disorganized meetings |

| Do's and Don'ts | **Do:** Come prepared, communicate clearly, take ownership<br><br>**Don't:** Make excuses and avoid responsibility |
|---|---|
| Strengths | **Key strengths:** Strategic thinking, planning<br><br>**How used:** Align goals, prioritize and plan work |
| Development Areas | **Working on:** Emotional intelligence<br><br>**Support me:** Honest feedback, ideas for improvement |
| Work Schedule | **Daily:** Mornings for focused planning times; afternoons for meetings |
| Personal | **Fun facts:** Enjoy camping and traveling to new places<br><br>**Recharge:** Outdoor activities |

## THE RACI CHART FOR ROLES AND RESPONSIBILITIES

Teams that perform at high levels have clarity in their roles and responsibilities. They know their lane and the lanes of their teammates. And when something shifts because of external or internal forces, they shift with it and make sure that shared understanding remains intact.

Well-defined roles create alignment and promote transparency, which results in better outcomes for customers and increased engagement for employees. Roles give us a sense of identity and provide focus.

Imagine a group of eight talented musicians who meet for the first time. Someone walks in and says, "Everyone, play your instrument." The sounds that followed would likely be discordant. This may sound silly, and you're thinking that no one does this. Yet we see this type of interaction happen in the workplace. A meeting occurs where a decision is made to do something, and then, automagically, the expectation is that a team miraculously forms itself, complete with a leader at the helm. Instead, it's more likely that little, if anything, gets done.

Without clearly defined roles and responsibilities, confusion ensues, leading to inefficiencies, conflicts, unnecessary stress, and frustrations. A powerful tool that brings clarity for defining roles and responsibilities is the RACI chart. RACI stands for responsible, accountable, consult, and inform.

- **Responsible:** The leader or team member responsible for completing a project task.
- **Accountable:** The person with final authority over the completion of that task or deliverable.
- **Consulted:** Someone with specific insights or expertise who the team will consult.
- **Informed:** A stakeholder who isn't directly involved but who should be regularly informed.

This tool is especially helpful when work involves more than one team with multiple handoff points. An example of how a RACI chart could be applied to an employee onboarding project follows:

| TASK/DELIVERABLE | HIRING MANAGER | HR TEAM | IT TEAM | NEW HIRE | MENTOR/BUDDY | DEPT. HEAD |
|---|---|---|---|---|---|---|
| Job Offer | A | R | – | – | – | – |
| Preemployment Paperwork | – | R | – | A | – | – |
| Company Orientation | C | R | – | – | – | A |
| Workstation Setup | A | – | R | – | – | – |
| Role-Specific Training | R | C | – | – | A | – |
| IT Security Training | – | – | R | A | – | – |
| Buddy Assignment | A | C | – | – | R | C |
| First Week Check-In | A | R | – | – | C | – |
| Ninety-Day Review | R | C | – | – | C | A |

In this example, roles are defined as follows:

- **Hiring manager:** Accountable for ensuring that the new hire is onboarded successfully, setting role expectations, and managing check-ins and reviews.

- **HR team:** Responsible for facilitating the onboarding process, including paperwork, orientation, compliance, and initial role-specific training.

- **IT team:** Responsible for setting up the new hire's workstation and accounts and for providing IT security training.

- **New hire:** Accountable for completing required trainings and paperwork and for participating in the onboarding process.

- **Mentor/buddy:** Responsible for helping the new hire acclimate to the company culture and acting as a resource for role-specific guidance.

- **Department head:** Consulted and informed about the new hire's progress, onboarding, and reviews.

Once the RACI chart has been drafted, each person who has a role in the project reviews it for accuracy, completeness, and agreement. After it has been finalized and communicated, role ambiguity should be minimal.

Clarity in roles and responsibilities guides team members toward common outcomes. Everyone knows their specific duties, what level of authority they have, and who they need to consult with or inform. This minimizes duplication of effort, avoids missing tasks that were unassigned, streamlines decision-making, and accelerates the work to be done. Communication, collaboration, and transparency improve across the team.

Imagine a workplace where your team members understand their roles and what is expected of them in terms of behavior and performance. Your team feels empowered to get things done. You don't waste time on rework or misunderstandings. The result is a team culture of trust, accountability, and high performance. Clear communication is the foundation—now it needs to be reinforced with effective feedback.

CHAPTER NINE

# FEEDBACK

**AN AIRPLANE IS OFF COURSE ABOUT 90 PERCENT** of the time due to changes in weather conditions, wind speed and direction, and turbulence. The plane's GPS takes these changing conditions into consideration and provides feedback to the autopilot on a regular basis; the pilot (or autopilot) then corrects to bring the plane back on course. The GPS doesn't view the feedback as good or bad; it's just the information that is needed to help steer the plane to its destination—no judgment, straightforward, and necessary.

If you want someone to fail, withhold feedback. We can't fix a problem that we don't know we have. As a leader, your ability to provide positive and constructive feedback to your team serves the same purpose as the GPS for an airplane—to keep them on track with behaviors, performance, and personal growth and development. Feedback is one of your most powerful tools for guiding the growth and success of your team. Whether it's positive reinforcement for a job well done or constructive feedback for improvement, feedback shapes behavior and performance.

How you provide feedback can make a significant difference in how your team functions, grows, and achieves results. It goes beyond pointing out strengths and weaknesses. Feedback helps you build trust and open communications with your team. When employees receive regular feedback, they know where they stand, what is expected of them, and how they can improve. This clarity helps prevent misunderstandings and aligns individual performance with the broader goals of the department and organization.

Let's look at tactics for providing feedback and how to use it constructively.

## POSITIVE REINFORCEMENT FEEDBACK

We all like positive feedback. Good leaders look for positive behaviors to reinforce desirable actions. For example, you have a meeting where most of the attendees show up a few minutes early or on time and several who join after the meeting has started. You could point out the latecomers and ask them to be on time for future meetings. Or a better approach is to provide positive feedback to those who were on time. "Thank you to those of you who were on time for the meeting. I really appreciate starting on time, since we have a lot to cover." That sends a message to both groups. The prompt ones like the recognition for being on time, and the late people know they've been called out indirectly.

Examples of positive behaviors that you'd want to recognize include:

- Proactive problem-solving, where team members take initiative to address issues without being asked
- Collaboration and teamwork, when individuals share information and go out of their way to help others succeed

- Flexibility and adaptability for employees who are open to change and adjust quickly to new priorities or handle unexpected situations calmly
- Effective communication, when a team member does a great job with a presentation or leading meetings
- Ownership and accountability, when team members take responsibility for their work, own mistakes, and work toward solutions without blame
- Customer focus for employees who go above and beyond to meet customer needs
- Creative thinking, when a team member brings new ideas or approaches to add value to the team.

Recognition of positive behaviors that you value helps set clear expectations for your team. Keep in mind that people mimic the leader, so these should also be traits that you model.

Maybe you're thinking this sounds like an everyone-gets-a-trophy approach. That's not what we're aiming for. Positive recognition should be for those instances when people are truly excelling, not just meeting job expectations. Let's examine when positive feedback is not appropriate by looking at a communication exchange between Isabelle, the leader, and Zach, one of her team members.

> Isabelle: "Zach, you did a really good job in that meeting."
> Zach: "Thank you. What did I do that you liked?"
> Isabelle: "You had an agenda, started it on time, and everyone participated."

At first glance, you might think this is good, positive feedback. However, what if the meeting didn't achieve the outcome or decisions needed? Was it a good meeting or just a meeting that started on time and everyone had a chance to talk? Unless this was Zach's first time running a meeting, this barely met meeting basics.

Instead, feedback that reinforces the importance of a well-run, successful meeting might look like this:

> Isabelle: "Zach, you did a great job running the meeting. People were prepared, the agenda was well organized, everyone participated, the requirements were well documented, and we made the needed decisions to move ahead. You skillfully navigated some challenging personalities and got to the decision everyone could agree on."

See the difference?

Match the praise with the impact. Authentic praise is effective because it highlights the significance of a person's efforts and its positive effects, reinforcing the behavior. On the contrary, superficial or insincere praise rings hollow and lacks credibility, losing its value to motivate or inspire. People value recognition that is meaningful and authentic. It demonstrates an understanding and appreciation of the efforts put forth.

Unfortunately, not all feedback is positive. Sometimes you need to address negative behaviors.

## CONSTRUCTIVE FEEDBACK

"Would you mind if I give you some feedback?" We've all heard this or some variation of it, and our first thought usually isn't, *Yes! I can hardly wait to hear you point out what I did wrong. Yippee!* Instead, our amygdala defaults to danger signals, and our emotion may be one of dread or fear.

As a leader, you want to help your team grow and develop, but constructive feedback tends to put most people on the defensive. Tips for providing constructive feedback include the following:

- **Talk in private.** Don't use a public forum to provide feedback on negative behaviors. No one wants to be called out in front of their peers or others.

- **Have empathy.** Understand that the individual's emotions may be fear or defensiveness. Feedback is meant to help someone become a better version of themselves; it's not to be used as an opportunity to put them down.

- **Provide authentic feedback.** Any feedback you offer should genuinely be meant to help the person you are talking with.

- **Be timely.** Minimize the time between the event and the feedback so that what happened is clear and everyone remembers what transpired.

- **Be specific.** Explain to the person specifically what was inappropriate about the behavior and let them know what is expected. Make it actionable.

- **Focus on behavior, not on the person.** Avoid making the feedback personal. If a team member is frequently late for meetings, a leader could say, "I've noticed that you've been late for meetings the past two weeks" versus "You don't seem very reliable since you're always late to meetings."

- **Balance positives and negatives.** Where possible, acknowledge things the person is doing that you like and then where they can improve. For example, if Brian tends to talk a lot in meetings or conversations, as the leader, you could say, "Brian, I love your enthusiasm for the project and your willingness to share with others. However, when we're in meetings, it's important for everyone to have a chance to speak and share their ideas. Meetings tend to go past our allotted time, and we aren't able to get through all the agenda items. Please be concise and ensure that others are also given an opportunity to offer their perspectives."

Even with the best of intentions, feedback can trigger fear and anger. Sometimes well-intentioned feedback doesn't go as planned, even when the other person agrees to hear it.

## FEEDBACK AND THE AMYGDALA HIJACK

I had back-to-back meetings with the relatively new president of a client company, Doug, where I was an adviser to the CEO. The first meeting we had together included the executive team. In that meeting, Doug had already decided to bring back a vendor that the sales VP had fired a year earlier for poor performance. Doug unilaterally decided to disregard the prior history and wanted to communicate his decision to the executives. The meeting didn't go well, as others disagreed with the decision and were confused as to the purpose of the meeting. Some thought the meeting was to discuss the vendor and others didn't even know why they had been invited. It was frustrating for everyone.

My weekly one-on-one meeting with Doug was scheduled right after the vendor meeting. He joined our video call and started ranting about the previous meeting and how he wasn't allowed to make decisions. He was frustrated with the executive team and his perceived lack of authority. When he finally took a breath, I asked if he was open to my thoughts on what might have made the prior meeting more successful. He said, "Yes, please! That meeting was a disaster." I began by saying that no one knew the context of the meeting and the expected outcomes.

That's about as far as I got before his face turned red, his neck veins popped out, and he raised his voice. "I'm tired of you telling people they need agendas, meeting context, and all that project management stuff."

I said, "Let's find another time to talk, as this conversation isn't serving either of us. We can regroup later."

Not all people take kindly to feedback, even when they've given you permission. I find that ending a heated conversation and reconvening later is a good tactic to use because it gives the other person time to calm down and reflect on the purpose of the call. Follow up later when they are in a better frame of mind and have had time to think about the situation.

Doug called me back later that day and apologized for his outburst. We had a more constructive conversation after that. After taking time to think about the meeting, he understood the other perspectives and decided to reverse his position on the vendor.

How do you react in contentious situations? Are you calm, cool, and collected, or do you feel your face start to turn red and then get angry and act in a way that you wish you could take back later? We've likely all been in meetings where the leader erupts and tempers flare. It's no fun and makes everyone uncomfortable, and little is achieved.

Feedback, both positive and negative, lays the groundwork for growth and professional course corrections for you and for your team. Constructive feedback, in particular, can be challenging.

## DIFFICULT CONVERSATIONS

Your neighbor's dog barks whenever it's outside, which is most of the time. It keeps you awake at night. You want to say something to the neighbor but are concerned that it might turn into a fight. Maybe it's better to suck it up and not say anything.

A friend promised to repay the money you loaned them after they get their first paycheck from a new job. It's been two months, and they haven't mentioned anything. How do you bring this up?

An older relative visits and starts to light up a cigarette in your house. Or maybe they stand outside to smoke but leave the door open. Do you say something to them?

Your job has gotten more demanding, and you need your significant other to start helping out more with household chores, day care drop-off and pickup, doctor appointments, and school events. In the past, they've said that their job is more important and that they don't have time. How do you handle it?

In the workplace, challenging situations arise on a seemingly daily basis that involve a difficult conversation, whether it's about low performance, personal hygiene, or inappropriate behaviors. If you struggle with whether to confront a situation or avoid it, you're not alone.

Lou Solomon, communications expert, reports that 69 percent of managers are uncomfortable communicating with employees. Over a third (37 percent) of managers are uncomfortable having to give feedback about employees' performance if they think the employee may respond negatively.[3]

Research by VitalSmarts shows that 72 percent of survey respondents provided examples when they or others failed to speak up when a peer didn't pull their weight. Sixty-eight percent reported a failure to address disrespect, and 57 percent didn't call out peers when they didn't comply with important workplace processes. Also included in the report is "every failure to have a tough conversation costs the organization approximately $7,500 and more than seven workdays."[4]

What do people do instead of having tough conversations? A report from Crucial Learning provides the following insights:

- 77 percent complain to others.
- 63 percent do extra or unnecessary work.
- 57 percent ruminate about the problem.
- 49 percent get mad.[5]

People spend approximately three hours a week working around conflicts, complaining to others, doing the work themselves, or figuring out how to solve problems that aren't theirs.

Why do people spend hours each week just to avoid what probably amounts to a ten-minute conversation? Part of our hesitancy to have difficult conversations dates to us being social animals—we want to be accepted and part of our tribe.

We don't want to start a fight, hurt someone's feelings, cause resentment, or damage a relationship.

In the book *Difficult Conversations*, authors Douglas Stone, Bruce Patton, and Sheila Heen write, "Delivering a difficult message is like throwing a hand grenade. Coated with sugar, thrown hard or soft, a hand grenade is still going to do damage. Try as you may, there's no way to throw a hand grenade with tact or to outrun the consequences. And keeping it to yourself is no better. Choosing not to deliver a difficult message is like holding on to a hand grenade once you've pulled the pin."[6]

That is a great analogy for difficult conversations. No one likes to have them, but they're still necessary.

When you don't have the needed hard conversations, you must deal with the high cost of this decision. First, you lose credibility and the respect of your team and peers. As the leader, you set the standards, and people will follow your example. Everyone already knows that there's an issue, and they wonder why you aren't addressing it. Second, the person who needs to hear the tough conversation isn't given an opportunity to improve. They can't grow if they're unaware that they're causing an issue. Third, you're wasting valuable time—time that could be spent helping the person or time you're spending complaining when you could be doing real work. Eventually, if left unresolved, employee morale, engagement, and motivation decrease when it is apparent there are no consequences for bad behavior. Lastly, as the leader, you may experience higher levels of anxiety or stress by delaying the conversation.

To quote Lee Cockerell from Disney, "A leader's job is to do what has to be done, when it has to be done, in the way it should be done whether you like it or not and whether they like it or not." There's not much ambiguity in what this means for having tough conversations.

## PREPARING FOR THE CONVERSATION

Now that you've decided to have that hard conversation, it's time to prepare for it. First and foremost, confirm that the behavior needing to be addressed is really an issue and not an emotional response. Detangle what is emotional from the real issue. People who are insecure or who are micromanagers may tend to think someone is going around them or trying to undermine them when in reality the other person is doing what they think is required. The conversation to be had is one of clarification.

Plan to meet with the person privately, in person, or via a video call. Prior to the meeting, be sure that you are ready, with a clear head and mindset. These meetings are likely the most important ones you have and warrant appropriate attention and preparation. Plan to go into the meeting with the assumption that the person had good motives, and expect a positive outcome. If you start the meeting assuming the worst, your body language and facial expressions will reflect that. The same is true if you go into the meeting with an open mind and a generous mindset.

Approach the conversation with curiosity or a problem-solving attitude rather than being punitive or wanting to win. Great leaders help people grow and become better, practicing tough love without crushing someone's confidence. If you have allowed a problem to fester, it's much more difficult to have the right mindset.

Before the meeting, determine a desired outcome for the conversation. Decide in advance what you want from the discussion to help keep the topics focused.

Be prepared to listen to what the other person has to say. Try to see things from their perspective and understand what they may be feeling. We all have life events that may detract from our work. The conversation may go in a different direction if you learn that the other person (or a family member) has a medical situation, is going through a divorce, or is experiencing some other event that requires attention. Taking care of someone through situations like these often results in long-term loyalty to the company.

As you think about the situation, is there a possibility that you may have played a role in it? For example, if one of your team members isn't doing what you expected, did you provide clear instructions and set realistic expectations, or did you just point them in a direction and expect them to figure it out? If your behavior could have affected the situation, be prepared to bring that up during the conversation.

Lastly, as you prepare for the discussion, practice it with another person if you don't have a lot of experience having difficult conversations.

## A FRAMEWORK FOR DIFFICULT CONVERSATIONS

The following is a framework for having difficult conversations that I find most helpful:

**Purpose:** Find a common purpose and get agreement on that.
- We both agree that completing this project on time is important, right?
- We both agree that we want to provide great service to our customers, right?
- We both agree that <fill in the blank>, right?

**Situation:** State the issue that you'd like to discuss.

- We need to talk about the comment you made in that last meeting.
- We need to discuss the quality/timeliness of your work products.
- We need to discuss the attitude of why things can't be done instead of looking for solutions.

**Impact:** State the impact that the behavior is having.

- Your frequent comments in meetings seem to be shutting others down, and we aren't getting the best thought leadership because of this.
- Being late on your deliverables is causing others to be late. Your team members are frustrated by the delays.
- Giving excuses about why things can't be done is eroding the department's credibility.

**Questions:** Ask for the other person's input and remember to *listen*.

- Do you see this differently?
- What can I do to help?
- What challenges are you dealing with?

**Outcome:** Agree on how behaviors will change in the future.

- I will make sure that others have a chance to offer their thoughts before I talk.
- We can assign another person to help get your deliverables back on track.
- I will work on my attitude and be better at finding solutions.

## DELIVER THE MESSAGE

Start the conversation with the issue at hand, following the framework. This is not the time for chitchat or for making small talk—go in and get to the point. As you work through the various steps in the conversation, remember to think about the role you may have played in the situation and bring this up. "I realize that I may not have been as clear as I should've been" or "I should've talked with you about this sooner." This will help defuse the situation and put the person more at ease.

Address the behavior, not the person. As Gandhi said, "Hate the sin, love the sinner." It's OK to use *love* and *hate* in the sentence. "I love how enthusiastic you are about the project but hate that you're often late for meetings. This sends the wrong message to the other team members who are punctual. What would help so that you're on time for meetings?"

Listen—really listen—to the response and don't interrupt. Hear where the person is coming from and validate where possible: "I can understand why you might feel this way." Actively listen and hear what is being said, even if you disagree with what they are saying. Ask for clarification, if needed: "Help me better understand that last part" or "Tell me more about this."

Ask what the person needs from you.

Continue to keep the conversation focused on the desired outcome, especially if the other person becomes defensive. If the conversation becomes heated or unproductive, it's best to hit pause and reconvene when the parties have had time to calm down and think more clearly.

After the conversation, as the leader, it's your job to follow up and ensure that the changes are being made. Acknowledge the positive behavior change for reinforcement. If the change doesn't stick, it's also your job to take appropriate action.

Great leaders have difficult conversations and follow through on the outcomes.

## EXAMPLES OF DIFFICULT CONVERSATIONS

Let's look at several situations requiring difficult conversations and how they may have gone without following a framework (1A) and then how the framework could help you better structure the conversation (1B).

### Example 1

Sheila and Greta are peers who both report into a director-level position. When that director left the company, both women applied for the role. After interviews, including external candidates, Sheila was promoted to the position of director, with Greta reporting to her. Greta had been with the company longer and was upset about not getting the promotion. She has had several conversations with team members that she was more qualified for the position than Sheila.

**Example 1A—The Conversation That Doesn't Go Well**

*Sheila:* "Greta, I've heard from several employees that you've been saying things about me behind my back and questioning my qualifications for this role. Why are you doing this? This isn't professional, and I don't appreciate it."

*Greta:* "Who told you that?"

*Sheila:* "It doesn't matter who told me. That's not the issue. The issue is that you're saying things behind my back that aren't true."

*Greta:* "Well, I'm just saying what everyone else is thinking! You're new to this position, and let's be honest, I've been here longer. I should've gotten the promotion, not you."

*Sheila:* "That's not the point! You're undermining my authority and making me look bad. You need to stop this gossip immediately, or we're going to have a bigger problem."

*Greta:* "You know what, Sheila? Maybe you should focus on proving you deserve the role rather than worrying about what I say."

*Sheila:* "This is exactly the kind of attitude that's causing problems, Greta. I'm not going to argue with you, but this can't continue."

The conversation ends with tension still high. Sheila feels unheard, and Greta is defensive and dismissive. No resolution or mutual understanding is reached, and the workplace tension likely remains unresolved.

**Example 1B: The Conversation Using the Framework**

*Sheila:* "Greta, I'd like to have a conversation with you. My goal is to maintain a positive working relationship and to ensure that we're both supporting each other and our teams in our roles. Can we agree that we both want this?" (Purpose)

*Greta:* "Yes, we definitely want to support the teams."

*Sheila:* "I know this promotion has been a significant change for both of us, and I want to make sure we're aligned moving forward. I've noticed some tension within the team recently, and I've heard from a few team members that you've expressed concerns about my qualifications for the new role. I want to make sure we address this directly because I value our working relationship." (Situation)

Greta starts to look defensive and crosses her arms, indicating that this might be an uncomfortable conversation. Sheila continues calmly.

*Sheila:* "Before we go any further, I want to make sure you know I really respect your experience and contributions to the team. I also want to hear your thoughts and feelings openly, without judgment. My goal here is to clear the air and find a way for us to work better together." (Questions)

*Greta:* "Well, it's been hard for me to accept that I wasn't promoted. I felt like I should have been considered for the role more seriously, and I guess I've been venting about it."

*Sheila:* "I completely understand how you feel. I want to share my perspective as well. When you've been saying things like I'm not ready for this role to others on the team, it's created some division. It's made it harder for me to build trust as the new leader, and it's also causing tension among team members. I'm concerned this could affect how we all work together going forward." (Impact)

*Greta:* "I didn't realize it was causing that much of an issue. I've just been frustrated, but I see how that could create more problems for you. Honestly, I just felt hurt because I thought I had a chance at that role too."

*Sheila:* "Thank you for sharing that with me. I can see how this has been difficult for you, and I really appreciate your honesty. It's important for me that we clear up any misunderstandings and work together to make sure the teams succeed."

*Sheila:* "Moving forward, I'd really like us to communicate directly if there's anything you're feeling or if you have concerns about my role. I want us to support each other and help the teams work closely together. Does that sound reasonable to you?" (Outcome)

*Greta:* "Yes, I think that's fair. I didn't mean to cause issues, and I'll be more mindful of how I express my feelings going forward. I'll come to you if I have concerns."

*Sheila:* "That's all I'm asking for. I know we can work

through this and be a strong team. Thanks for your openness, Greta."

In the second example, Sheila stays calm, notices the change in Greta's body language with the crossed arms, and tells her that she respects her experience and contributions. Sheila stays focused on specific behaviors and clearly explains the impact. This allows Greta to respond more positively. The conversation ends with agreement to work toward a common goal.

## Example 2

Mark is frustrated that John, one of his managers, has not taken action to terminate Rich, a low performer who has been on a performance plan for several months. John hasn't fired anyone before and also feels sorry for Rich, who is a single father of three kids. Several of John's employees have gone to Mark to complain that they're tired of having to do Rich's work and of John making excuses for him. They've asked to be transferred to another project.

### Example 2A: The Conversation That Doesn't Go Well

*Mark:* "John, we need to talk about Rich. I'm frustrated that you haven't taken action to terminate him even though he's been on a performance plan for months. What's going on?"

*John:* "I know, but it's not that easy. Rich is a single father of three kids. I feel bad for him."

*Mark:* "That's not an excuse, John. The rest of the team is picking up his slack, and they're getting tired of it. Some have even come to me asking for transfers."

*John:* "Well, I'm doing the best I can. Firing someone is tough, and I've never had to do it before."

*Mark:* "It's your responsibility as a manager to make these difficult decisions. You're letting Rich drag down the whole team. I'm losing patience."

*John:* "You don't understand the situation. It's complicated."

*Mark:* "Complicated or not, this can't continue. You need to step up and deal with it, or I'll have to take over."

This conversation ends with tension still high. Mark feels that John is making excuses, and John feels unsupported in making a difficult decision. The problem remains unresolved, and frustration builds on both sides.

### Example 2B: The Conversation Using the Framework

*Mark:* "We need to talk about team member performance. Do we both agree that we need to have the best talent on our team? A-players?" (Purpose)

*John:* "Yes, we do for sure."

*Mark:* "John, I'd like to talk about Rich's situation and your team's morale."

*John:* "OK. What's on your mind?"

*Mark:* "Over the past few weeks, several team members have come to me with concerns about having to take on Rich's work." (Situation) "They mentioned that they feel like you've been making excuses for him, and some have even asked to be transferred to another project." (Behavior) "This has created frustration within the team, and it's affecting their motivation and productivity." (Impact)

*John:* "I didn't realize it was affecting them that much. I just feel really bad for Rich, you know? He's got kids, and firing him would be hard."

*Mark:* "I completely understand how you feel. It's never easy to let someone go, especially when personal circumstances are involved. But I want to remind you that the rest of the team is also feeling the weight of this situation. They're starting to lose confidence in the fairness of the workload, and it's creating tension within the group."

*John:* "I can see that now. I've been avoiding it, but I realize it's unfair to the others."

*Mark:* "It's tough, I know, and I'm here to support you through it. Let's focus on what we can do to help Rich transition out in a way that's respectful while also ensuring that the rest of the team isn't being overburdened. Maybe we could help him with job placement services or a severance package to ease the situation. How do you feel about moving forward with that plan?" (Outcome)

*John:* "I think that would help. It would make me feel better about the decision, and I can see it's the right move for the team."

*Mark:* "Great. Let's work together on this, and I'm here if you need help with the process."

Using the framework, Mark stays focused on the common goal, specific situation, impact, and outcome, making the conversation less accusatory and more constructive. He acknowledges John's feelings while guiding him toward a fair and necessary resolution.

## Example 3

Holly is a manager who is frustrated by the surprise of missed deliverables from Steve, the lead data analyst on her team. Holly has been informed that executives have decided to bring in an outside consultant to see why this project is so late. Steve is a valued member of the team but has seemed distant over the past several months. He's a very private person and doesn't like talking about his personal life. A few months ago, his wife was in a car accident, and he's needed to take on additional work at home with the kids while his wife recovers. He hasn't told anyone at work about this.

## Example 3A: The Conversation That Doesn't Go Well

*Holly:* "You don't seem to be getting your job done, and it's really slowing down the project."

*Steve:* "It's not my fault. The file that came in was missing data, and I had to go back to the client to get it. Their IT shop was really slow, and it took them forever to get it to me."

*Holly:* "How long did it take to get the missing data?"

*Steve:* "Three weeks."

*Holly:* "How many times did you follow up?"

*Steve:* "Maybe twice, but it's not my job to babysit the client. They should know better."

*Holly:* "I need you to do whatever it takes to keep this project on schedule."

*Steve:* "I understand, but you don't know what's going on behind the scenes. It's not like I'm slacking off."

*Holly:* "Well, if there's something going on, you should have brought it up before. Now it's too late, and we're all paying the price for it. You need to get your act together."

*Steve:* "I don't appreciate being blamed for everything. I'm working as hard as I can, and this feels really unfair."

*Holly:* "You're a key member of the team, Steve, but if you can't meet deadlines, we're going to have a problem. I need this fixed—and fast."

*Steve:* "Fine. I'll figure it out, but I don't see how bringing in a consultant is going to help."

In this conversation, Holly's frustration escalates the situation, making Steve defensive and reluctant to share what's really going on. They both walk away feeling misunderstood, with no resolution to the problem, and Steve's personal struggles remain hidden.

## Example 3B: The Conversation Using the Framework

*Holly:* "Hi, Steve. We need to talk about the delays in the project schedule. Do we both agree that this project is a very important one for the company that will improve our efficiencies and costs?" (Purpose)

*Steve:* "Yes, it is."

*Holly:* "Do we agree that your role and skills are critical for this project to be successful?" (Purpose)

*Steve:* "Yes. I know that a lot is riding on me."

*Holly:* "You're a valued member of the team, and I know this is a complex project. The schedules are tight, people are working long hours, and tensions are running high. It's no fun. However, it seems that you've been late on several of your deliverables, and I'm not getting any advance notice that we aren't going to hit our milestones. These surprises are causing us to have a lot of scrutiny by the executive team. The executive sponsor has contracted with an external consultant to come in next week to do a project review. Although I know this is a high-stress project, I can't be blindsided when we miss dates." (Situation) "Is there something more going on that I might not be aware of? Is there anything happening that's making it difficult for you to keep up with the workload?"

(Questions)

*Steve:* "Well . . . to be honest, yeah. My wife was in a car accident a few months ago, and since then I've been handling everything at home. It's been really hard to balance things, but I didn't want to bring it up at work."

*Holly:* "I'm really sorry to hear about your wife, Steve. That sounds incredibly tough. I appreciate you telling me, and I completely understand why it's been difficult for you to manage everything."

*Steve:* "Thanks. I've been trying to push through, but it's just been a lot lately."

*Holly:* "I can only imagine. Let's figure out a plan that works for you and the team. Maybe we can redistribute some of the workload for now, and I can support you in getting things back on track. I want to make sure we're helping you as much as possible." (Outcome)

*Steve:* "I'd really appreciate that. I've been feeling overwhelmed but didn't know how to bring it up."

*Holly:* "I'm glad you shared this with me. We'll get through this together. Let's talk about how we can adjust things to relieve some of that pressure."

Using the framework, Holly is empathetic and focuses on the goal, situation, and impact without placing blame. This approach helps Steve feel safe enough to open up about his personal challenges, and they can work together to find a solution that supports both Steve and the project.

Frameworks aren't a silver bullet, but they do provide a structure you can use to think about how to best approach various types of difficult conversations. As mentioned earlier, humans are messy. Conversations can go in many different directions and often turn defensive. If you can't talk them off the ledge or they are no longer listening, you may want to pause the conversation and return to it when the other person is in a better frame of mind.

Maybe you're thinking that you just simply want to avoid the hard conversation. It's too uncomfortable. If this describes you, the following tactics may make it easier:

- **Reframe your mindset.** Instead of focusing on how hard it's going to be, concentrate on the benefits of having the conversation, such as building trust with your team, solving problems, and removing the friction caused by inaction. Think about the bigger picture of your team's well-being. Remind yourself that avoiding the situation likely has had a negative effect on the whole team.

- **Be prepared.** You have a framework available to use. Gather the facts and data to stay objective. If you're feeling anxious, practice deep breathing exercises to help you stay calm and centered.

- **Rehearse.** Practice the hard discussion with another person until you feel confident enough that you're ready for the real conversation. Document key points that you want to make. Think about scenarios of how the conversation could go.

- **Be empathetic.** Put yourself in the other person's shoes and how they may see the situation. When you show you care, it's more likely the other person will be more open to a productive discussion.

- **Actively listen.** You've seen active listening a few times now. It applies to difficult conversations as well. Allow the other person opportunities to talk and share their perspectives. Acknowledge their feelings and perspectives to help ease tension.

- **Ask for help.** If you have a particularly difficult conversation with someone who is known to be unruly, you may want to ask your manager or someone from HR to attend the meeting. This especially applies if this is one of the first times you've been in this situation.

Remember that it's more important to take action to correct a situation than to let it linger, because it will likely cause far more damage to the team, morale, engagement, and performance.

## PERFORMANCE REVIEWS

Some leaders do a great job of providing feedback on a regular basis, which I support. No one should have to wait six to twelve months to know if they're doing a good job. I understand that HR wants performance reviews conducted at certain intervals to formally document feedback. In my opinion, when they are done annually or semiannually, the feedback may be outdated. When spanning several months of performance, the focus is usually more on recent events than over the performance period, leading to limited and/or biased perspectives.

I've been in several companies where HR departments send out performance review emails with little to no training and sometimes without sufficient notice to do a thorough job.

Often no guidance or calibration is provided on how to evaluate people. Some managers tend to give higher ratings than others; some ratings are biased, depending on how well someone is liked or who they are related to. Some companies limit the number of employees who can receive an *exceeds* rating. Others don't do a good job of explaining what is needed for each rating. Some reviewers focus primarily on an employee's weaknesses instead of their strengths. Sound familiar?

This is why setting clear expectations, assigning performance measures, and providing feedback are so important. Everyone should know what is expected of them and how they are meeting the expectations. It shouldn't be a mystery or cause undue stress. Feedback should be given frequently.

Here are tips to help when performance reviews come around. Keep in mind that these are not meant to replace HR policies but to augment how you, as the leader, can provide effective performance reviews:

- Be objective when evaluating an employee's performance against the measures and expectations that you set for them (you did this, right?). With specific measures, the evaluation becomes more quantitative and qualitative. Did you complete four book studies with your team? Did you meet or exceed the expected number of tickets resolved each week? Did customer satisfaction increase by two percentage points?

- Provide feedback, positive and constructive, regularly, not just at review time. No one should be surprised during an annual review if they've been given timely feedback throughout the year.

- Focus on outcomes, not on how many hours someone has worked. If you have an employee who works sixty hours a week but does a lousy job, don't reward the hours.

- Focus primarily on an employee's strengths, not on their weaknesses. For example, if a person has an introverted personality style and likes analysis, but you have them in a sales role where they're measured on how many new customers they bring in, that's likely a strike against you, not them. Continue to find ways to develop employee strengths—it's a win-win for everyone.

- Encourage two-way communication, allowing the employee to share their perspectives, challenges, and goals during the review.

- Be specific in your feedback during the performance review to avoid ambiguity. Provide suggestions that are actionable, relevant, and achievable. For example, suggest a specific training class or books to help with growth areas.

- At the end of the review, check for alignment. Document any follow-up activities for future discussions.

Combining these tips with the upfront work of expectation setting, performance measures, one-on-one meetings, and ongoing feedback makes an employee review process so much easier and more effective.

This section on effective communication covers a lot of

ground and tactics. It may seem like communication requires a lot of work. You're right, it does. The good news is that you don't have to do everything all at once. Start with small steps and implement the tools and frameworks that you feel comfortable with to start building small wins each day.

Awareness

Effective Communication

Lead by Example

High-Performing Teams

Exceptional Results

Productivity Habits

# PART FOUR

# PRODUCTIVITY HABITS

We must all suffer from one of two pains:
the pain of discipline or the pain of regret.
The difference is discipline weighs ounces
while regret weighs tons.

**—JIM ROHN**

**IN TODAY'S FAST-PACED,** ever-changing world, there's no shortage of work to get done. Most people feel overwhelmed, often ending the workday with few accomplishments to show for it. They've been pulled into one meeting after another; interrupted by calls, texts, and chat messages; and had little time to get the "real" work done. They go home frustrated, mentally exhausted, and feeling even further behind.

Yet other people seem to get a lot more work done, leave at 5:00 p.m., and get promotions.

How do they do it? Great leaders don't get it all done—they get the highest-priority work done. They do this by focusing on the most important work, establishing routines, and putting systems in place to standardize and automate as much as possible.

## CHAPTER TEN
# THE IMPORTANCE OF FOCUS

**ALEX STARTS HIS DAY** with a familiar ritual: The alarm goes off on his smartphone beside the bed. He hits snooze a couple of times, and then, instead of getting up, he scrolls through emails and social media feeds. He decides to respond to a few of the messages and comment on a couple of posts before rolling out of bed. The short time he had planned to spend on his phone has now become an hour, and panic sets in as he realizes he's late for work. He dresses quickly, skips breakfast, and heads out the door. Alex's day is derailed before it even begins.

Can you relate? This happens to all of us. Social media, marketing and advertising, and other companies employ large numbers of people whose sole purpose is to figure out how to get your attention, to create an addiction to your electronic devices and applications. The goal is to make the interaction sticky.

Digital addiction is one of, if not the greatest, distractions in the workplace (and home), making it nearly impossible for many people to focus for more than a few minutes at a time. Darren Hardy, author and success coach, refers to digital distractions as weapons of mass distraction.

A survey conducted by Review.org of people eighteen years of age and older about their phone habits revealed that, in

2023, Americans checked their phones 144 times a day, with an average of four and a half hours a day of screen time. Eighty-nine percent checked their phones within the first ten minutes of waking up. About half the time (52 percent), people checked their phones during business hours.[1]

How often do you check your phone? Do you look at it during meetings when you should be paying attention? Do you feel like part of you is missing if you go to the bathroom and don't take your phone? What is your average weekly phone screen time?

## DISTRACTIONS AND HOW TO MINIMIZE THEM

A study conducted at the University of California at Irvine reports that it takes twenty-three minutes on average for a knowledge worker to regain their focus after an interruption. Coauthor Gloria Mask defines an interruption as one that requires thinking, one that makes you take your focus off a task and apply it to something else.[2] For example, if someone interrupts you with a question about what they need to present at a meeting that requires you to stop what you're doing and think about the meeting purpose, other meeting topics, and help them prepare for their part, the cognitive penalty is high. If someone stops by and asks what time everyone is meeting for happy hour, the impact is much less.

Consider the effect on productivity for a software engineer who is contemplating how to solve a problem. She may be weighing several alternatives and thinking through each one when the interruption occurs. If this lasts for longer than two or three minutes, she will spend almost half an hour ramping up her thought process to get it back to where it was before the interruption.

Think about the impact that three-minute interruptions could have on team productivity, not to mention errors. Five interruptions a day when working on cognitive tasks translates into almost two hours of additional time needed to ramp back up to the same level of thought. It's no wonder so many people leave work each day wondering what they accomplished.

It gets worse. David Rock, author of *Your Brain at Work*, describes how distractions are not only frustrating but also exhausting.[3] Regaining the thought process after an interruption requires energy, which decreases with each interruption. The more you're interrupted, the less energy you have, which equals less capacity to understand things, make decisions, recall needed information, or memorize things for long-term memory. As a result, you could make mistakes on important work or lose the ability to come up with great ideas and insights.

I want to emphasize the Jim Rohn quote at the beginning of this section: "We must all suffer from one of two pains: the pain of discipline or the pain of regret. The difference is discipline weighs ounces while regret weighs tons."

Discipline is one of those things that is often easier said than done. We know that we need to eat nutritious foods, exercise regularly, and get plenty of sleep for better health; wake up early to have a productive start to our day; limit screen time and avoid social media distractions; and stay organized by eliminating clutter in our workspace. But we don't always do that. To quote Jim Rohn again, "What's easy to do is also easy not to do." Simple tasks can be readily neglected because they require minimal effort to avoid doing them.

When it comes to leadership, self-discipline is a prerequisite. If you can't lead yourself, it will be difficult to lead others. Remember that people mimic the leader and do as they see (not as they hear). Let's look at several tactics you can put into practice to help improve focus for yourself and for your team.

## ROUTINES HELP YOU WIN THE DAY

As described by Alex's story at the beginning of this chapter, the morning routine for many people has them feeling behind and out of control all day long. For most people, the day will be won or lost based on their morning or evening habits. Highly productive leaders have a routine to start or end their day, so they actively choose how to manage their time instead of being reactive.

Benjamin Spall, author of *My Morning Routine: How Successful People Start Every Day Inspired*, writes that although the biggest predictor of success is simply having a steady routine, the most successful people in his book wake up before 6:00 a.m.[4] Apple CEO Tim Cook starts his morning at 3:45 a.m. Bill McNabb, chairman of Vanguard Group, is up by 5:00 a.m. and at his desk by 6:15 a.m. Even Scott Adams, creator of *Dilbert*, wakes up as early as he can, usually between 4:00 a.m. and 6:00 a.m.

Robin Sharma, humanitarian and author of *The 5 AM Club: Own Your Morning, Elevate Your Life*, believes that rising by 5:00 a.m. when the world is quiet is the best time to ground ourselves and get focused for the day. He uses the first hour of his day to exercise, meditate, and learn, each in twenty-minute blocks of time. Sharma writes, "To perform like the top 5 percent, we need to stop acting like the 95 percent."[5]

A morning or evening routine is a great tactic for success that you want in your leadership toolbox.

An example of a morning routine might look like this:

- Wake up early (e.g., between 5:00 a.m. and 6:00 a.m.).
- Spend ten to fifteen minutes on a mindfulness or meditation practice.
- Exercise for twenty to thirty minutes (this could be a quick workout and/or stretching).
- Eat a healthy breakfast.
- Review goals and priorities for the week or day.
- Check for important emails or messages.

Routines are not a one-size-fits-all practice. Each person should do what works for them. I like to start my day early, between 5:00 a.m. and 5:30 a.m. and spend fifteen to twenty minutes listening to a guided meditation (I have to use a guided meditation because it's too hard for me to concentrate if I'm left to focus on my breathing). I usually exercise first thing in the morning and listen to a video or podcast so that I can get my personal development time done at the same time I'm working out. After exercising, I review my weekly or daily goals to plan my day. After breakfast, I set aside three hours each morning to work on the most cognitive tasks, usually writing, developing course materials, planning for key meetings, and the like. My brain is more alert in the mornings before the day gets started and has more cognitive horsepower for thinking.

Some of you may be thinking, *But I'm not a morning person!* or, like my sisters, *My house would need to be on fire before I'd get up that early!* I understand that it's not easy to rise early in the morning. If that describes you, then try adjusting a little at a time. Consider going to bed fifteen minutes earlier each night and getting up fifteen minutes earlier. The good news is that you don't need to instantly start getting up early. You can ease into it. Twice a year, most of us adjust to daylight saving time changes within a day or two.

Great leaders don't like getting up early any more than anyone else, but they do it anyway. They make it a habit, so it gets easier. For me, if I sleep later than 6:00 a.m., I feel like I'm playing catch-up for the rest of the day.

If getting up earlier to establish a productive morning routine is out of the question, consider having an evening routine. Reflect on what went well during the day, what was accomplished and what wasn't, and plan out priorities and work for the next day. Determine how often and when to get in exercise. Perhaps do a meditation or mindfulness exercise just before going to bed. The key is to establish routines to spend focused, uninterrupted time planning the most important activities to help win the day, being proactive versus reactive.

Do what works for you.

## POWER BLOCKS FOR FOCUSED TIME

Productive leaders set aside blocks of time when there are no interruptions—cell phones are turned off, the smartwatch is off, no meetings are scheduled, and all interruptions are put on hold. The length of focused time is usually one to two hours. If possible, try to have one to two blocks of focused time each day.

Most people do their best thinking and work early in the morning, before the monkey brain wakes up and the distractions begin. Decide the night before what you want to work on during your first block of time. That keeps you focused, and you don't have to think about what you want to do when you get up. The key is to keep your monkey brain sleeping for as long as possible. Close all the computer windows except the one you're working on. If you need to search for something on the internet, close the search window once you're done.

At first, having even one focused block of time a day for an hour might seem impossible. Maybe you don't think you have time. Or you feel overwhelmed and don't think you can spare even one hour. Start a little at a time. If you begin getting up fifteen minutes earlier, you can use that fifteen minutes to help plan your day.

Start with only one focused time block the first week and increase the duration or frequency over time. Quality thinking time pays huge dividends and is key to getting past being overwhelmed as a leader.

Every person I coach implements focused blocks of time, and they all report how much work they get done during that interval.

You can also implement power blocks of time for your team. Set designated times when no one is interrupted. No meetings are scheduled, chat messages are turned off, and email replies happen after the time block.

One of my clients provides underwriting services for home loans. The underwriting process can be quite complex, depending on the type of loan. Changes to regulations are not uncommon, and every loan applicant has different financial information. Underwriters were constantly interrupted by loan officers asking questions about other loan statuses or what information was needed. We set aside blocks of time designated for underwriting, with the underwriting manager fielding calls and questions to continue moving things along. Productivity went up and errors went down after implementing focused time.

Another client, a technology group, was dealing with team members who were constantly bombarded with chats or with people stopping by to ask a question to circumvent the trouble-ticketing system. To minimize disruptions, this team set blocks of time for focused work by working from home early in the mornings, reserving small conference rooms, and wearing headsets. Leaders communicated the importance of using the ticketing system to track common problems so that they could be proactive by developing better training or onboarding and building a knowledge base for use by everyone. Team members professionally redirected the interrupters to the ticketing system, explaining why following the process was important.

## OFFICE HOURS

If you manage a large team, you're likely interrupted several times a day. If in the office, people tend to stop by to ask a quick question, usually ones that are longer than three minutes and derail your train of thought. If hybrid, chat messages or emails likely come in that need your attention at some point.

In addition to the usual do-not-disturb features, you can help organize the nonurgent interruptions by establishing office hours, like professors do at college. Designate a time when team members can drop in to ask questions, either in person or via a video call.

I implemented office hours for one of the contracts I managed after spending the first hour and a half saying good morning and chatting with people who stopped by my office first thing. I let everyone know that I very much appreciated the morning greeting but couldn't afford to spend that much time on it. A thirty-minute time designated for quick questions or updates worked well. I still felt like I had an open-door policy but wasn't constantly interrupted. Employees could continue to schedule appointments if other meeting times were not sufficient or call my cell phone if something was urgent that needed immediate attention.

## REMOVE SOCIAL MEDIA FROM YOUR PHONE

I can hear you now. *Janet is a heretic to think I'm going to take social media off my phone.* Most people I know feel that way. As mentioned earlier, many companies make a lot of money by knowing how to best distract you. When you see messages waiting for you on a social platform, it's so tempting—just a quick sneak peek that turns into a much longer time.

I removed all social media from my phone and still survived. I designate a time at the end of the day for social media and have found that, over time, I may check it only once a week. The exceptions to this are when I post a question to a particular group or run surveys to get information. My productive time has increased by several hours a week since taking this action.

Most likely, you aren't going to remove social media from your phone. I recommend it but am not so naive as to think you're going to delete the apps just because you read this. Instead, could you limit the number of times you check it each day? Or set aside time once or twice a day that's specifically designated for social media?

## THE ILLUSION OF MULTITASKING

"NTSB: SNAPCHAT POST CAUSED FATAL DISTRACTION" read the headline of a safety article posted on the Aircraft Owner and Pilots Association website. The National Transportation Safety Board (NTSB) found that the pilot was distracted by posting to social media in flight during a low-altitude pipeline patrol. The airplane struck one of the cables attached to the radio tower in Saint Louis, Michigan, killing the twenty-three-year-old pilot.

"Based on the known information, it is likely the pilot was distracted while he used his mobile device in the minutes before the accident and did not maintain an adequate visual lookout to ensure a safe flight path to avoid the radio tower and its guy wires," the NTSB stated in the final report. "Contributing to the accident," the agency continued, "was the pilot's unnecessary use of his mobile device during the flight, which diminished his attention/monitoring of the airplane's flight path."[6]

Two people reported that the pilot posted a Snapchat video that showed the terrain ahead of the aircraft while it was five to ten miles southeast of the accident site, approximately thirty-five seconds before the accident.

Not only does social media adversely affect our productivity, but when trying to multitask using social media, it can prove fatal.

Some people tout how good they are at multitasking, almost like a badge of honor. Of course, these are the same people who ask you to repeat what was said earlier, didn't catch their action items, and caused you to go back and provide the context. Or maybe they just crashed.

Multitasking is only successful when a cognitive (thinking) task is done with a task that is habitual, such as taking a walk. Even then, the ability to do both is not optimal. How many times have you stepped off a sidewalk or tripped over something while walking and texting? Or missed your exit while driving and talking on your phone? It's not possible for our brains to do two cognitive tasks at the same time. We may think that's what we're doing, but it's really task switching when more than one cognitive task is being done.

A study done by Harold Pashler showed that when a person attempts two cognitive tasks at once, their cognitive capacity drops. Working on two tasks at once took longer and resulted in more errors.[7] When accuracy is important, like landing an airplane, trying to multitask is a really bad idea.

Shifting attention from one task to another burns up oxygenated glucose, the fuel needed by your brain to stay focused. Task switching throughout the day quickly depletes this fuel and leaves you feeling more stressed and exhausted with few accomplishments.

Research by Joshua Rubenstein, David Meyer, and Jeffrey Evans showed that switching between tasks can cost as much as 40 percent of a person's productive time.[8] Think about this for a minute. Almost half your time is wasted when you switch between tasks all day. Could you use an extra fifteen to twenty hours a week to get more done? Stop task switching and instead implement focused blocks of time to work on one thing at a time to get more done than you might imagine.

Multitasking doesn't just waste time. It increases mistakes, adds stress, and leaves you feeling scattered instead of feeling like you've accomplished work of value. Before you can fix it, though, you need to know if it's actually a problem for you.

The following is a self-assessment you can complete to determine whether you tend to multitask. Each statement can be rated on a scale of 1 to 5 (1 = Never, 2 = Rarely, 3 = Sometimes, 4 = Often, 5 = Always):

| STATEMENT | RATING |
|---|---|
| 1. I often find myself switching between multiple tasks without fully finishing one. | |
| 2. I keep multiple browser tabs, documents, or tools open and alternate between them frequently. | |
| 3. During meetings, I check emails and messages or work on other tasks. | |
| 4. I feel like I am always juggling several things at once, without focusing fully on any one thing. | |
| 5. When a new task comes up, I often jump to it even if I haven't completed my current task. | |
| 6. I feel the need to respond to emails or messages immediately, even when working on other important tasks. | |
| 7. I have difficulty finishing tasks by the end of the day because I've worked on several things simultaneously. | |
| 8. I find it hard to set aside uninterrupted time for deep, focused work. | |

| | |
|---|---|
| 9. I feel mentally drained by the end of the day from having to constantly switch between tasks. | |
| 10. I sometimes miss deadlines or produce lower-quality work because I've tried to do too many things at once. | |
| 11. I find it hard to ignore notifications or distractions when I'm in the middle of working on something important. | |
| 12. I frequently multitask during conversations or meetings rather than giving them my full attention. | |
| 13. I feel less productive, even though I am working on multiple tasks throughout the day. | |
| 14. I find it hard to delegate tasks because I feel I need to handle many things at the same time. | |
| 15. I feel overwhelmed by having too many tasks competing for my attention. | |
| **Total Score** | |

Scoring interpretation:

- **15 to 30 (low multitasking tendency):** You rarely multitask and are likely good at focusing on one task at a time. You may already practice effective time management and prioritize deep work.

- **31 to 60 (moderate multitasking tendency):** You sometimes multitask, but it doesn't seem to be a constant habit. However, there may be opportunities to improve your focus and reduce task switching.

- **61 to 75 (high multitasking tendency):** You often multitask, which may be negatively affecting your productivity and stress levels. Consider adopting the strategies in this chapter to minimize distractions and improve focus.

How did you score? Remember, small changes over time compound into phenomenal results.

## SAYING YES TO SOMETHING MEANS SAYING NO TO SOMETHING ELSE

We all have the same twenty-four hours in a day and 365 days a year. Time is our most precious and scarcest commodity. Some of the greatest leaders say that they are prouder of what they said no to than what they said yes to. Warren Buffett said that for every one hundred ideas that were brought to him, he said no to ninety-eight of them. Steve Jobs quickly shut down all but a few products when he took over at Apple for the second time, leading it from the brink of bankruptcy to the third-largest Fortune 500 company.

Every time we say yes to something, we are saying no to something or someone else. Being part of a tribal species, it's hard to say no to others, especially to a higher-up. We tend to agree to just about everything suggested because we want to be liked or because we don't want to disappoint someone.

Perhaps you may feel like the extra work is key to getting the next promotion. Or you may fear that you won't be viewed as a team player if you say no.

Organization leaders seem to expect employees to do more and more. We've all heard that we need to do more with less. You're likely asked to take on more work when you already have a full load.

When asked to take on unplanned work, this is a great time to put into practice the emotional intelligence you learned about in chapter 6. Rather than immediately responding to the request, you have an opportunity to hit pause and think about it. You could say, "Thank you for bringing this up. Let me look at my scheduled work and get back to you later today or tomorrow. Would that be OK?" This gives you time to think through the impact of the additional work request and prepare a thoughtful response.

You then want to analyze the request using a few filters. First and foremost, is the work aligned with my goals and priorities? Do I have available resources? What would the impact be on existing work commitments and deliverables? Do I or my team have the right skill sets? Would this work provide additional growth opportunities for myself or my team members? What would be the effect on work-life balance if I or a team member agreed to do this work? Do I have clarity on the scope of work that is being requested?

Consider several scenarios where saying no is appropriate.

When you're asked to do work that isn't aligned with your goals, you can reply, "Before committing to this work, I'd like to ensure that it aligns with our team's goals and objectives. Let's review how this fits into our strategic priorities to ensure that we're spending our time and resources on the right work."

If your schedule and that of your team are already at capacity, you could say, "I'd love to do this work, but my team doesn't have bandwidth for the next two months. Taking on more work right now would compromise our deliverables and work that's already been promised."

Perhaps you're asked to do work that was not included in your or your team's priority list. Things pop up unexpectedly that need to get done. In this situation, you could say, "Let's review the current work and see if there are items that could be put on hold temporarily so that I can focus on the work you're asking me to do." The important thing is to stop adding work to an already full plate. Instead, balance the work with the available resources. Otherwise, it's like getting pecked to death by a duck.

If you're asked to do work but you don't have the right skill set, you can say, "I'm not the right person for this work, and it would take me a while to ramp up. John is a better fit for this. Let's talk with him." If you're known for figuring things out, you become an easy target to pile work on.

Sometimes you may get an unrealistic request from someone higher up. If your boss asks you to develop a business case for a new product idea in two days, that's probably not enough time. You can reply, "It's not possible to have a useful business case in two days. However, what I can do is have a rough draft of the first two sections in that time frame." Or you could ask what areas are the most important.

Remember, when you say yes to something, you are saying no to something else. That something else could be missing a key deliverable date or burning you and your team out. The best leaders are masters of the polite no, managing the priorities and workload of their teams and themselves.

## DELEGATION DRIVES SUCCESS

Richard was the manager of a team of financial analysts in one of my client companies. He had been a senior financial analyst for several years and had been recently promoted to the leadership role. He was a master at spreadsheets and loved working with them. In his new position, he continued to be the primary person crunching numbers, gathering data from the financial systems, and talking with sales leaders. He worked long hours and proudly displayed his spreadsheets to executives. What he didn't do was develop his team to take over this work so that he had more time to spend on being strategic. When I asked Richard why he continued to own the spreadsheets and analysis instead of training his team, he said, "It's faster for me to do it, and I like doing them. The team has other things they can work on."

Ram Charan, Steve Drotter, and Jim Noel, authors of *The Leadership Pipeline: How to Build the Leadership-Powered Company*, write, "It's one thing to figure out what needs to be done and who needs to do it; it's quite another, and much more psychologically difficult, to let go of work that you were trained to do and that has helped you become successful."[9]

While writing this book, I interviewed several C-suite executives. One of the questions I asked was this: "What are the primary reasons why mid-level managers don't progress into senior- and executive-level positions?" Responses almost always included the inability to delegate and lead through others. Without delegating, you become a bottleneck and can't scale. Richard will likely retire as a manager of financial analysts, several of whom will leave because of growth limitations under him, unless he can be convinced to become more strategic in leveraging his position as a leader and start teaching others.

If delegation doesn't come easily for you, you're not alone. Maybe you think you're the only one who can perform the work to your standard. Or it will take you longer to train someone else than to just do the work yourself. Perhaps you feel guilty adding more work for your team members. As the leader, it's not your job to do it all; it's your job to get it all done. Remember that hoarding work doesn't scale, limits productivity, and ultimately holds back the organization.

|  | Urgent | Not Urgent |
|---|---|---|
| **Important** | Do it right away | Schedule a time to do it later |
| **Not Important** | Delegate | Delete—remove unnecessary tasks |

Delegating work within a team is more than just distributing tasks—it's a strategic tool to optimize the collective skills and potential of the entire team, promoting growth and trust. Delegation not only lightens the load of the leader to focus on higher-value work but also improves productivity. It plays to the strengths of team members and promotes skill development. With cross-functional training, work can be assigned to more than just one person, mitigating the risks of being dependent on one individual.

Let's look at how you can use the Eisenhower Matrix, created by former US president Dwight Eisenhower and popularized by legendary leadership thinker Stephen R. Covey, to help decide what to delegate.

What tasks should a leader delegate? We can use the matrix to help us decide.

- **Urgent and important:** Assign someone to work closely with you or delegate with close oversight.
- **Not urgent and important:** This is a growth opportunity to delegate to others and empower them.
- **Urgent and not important:** Delegate entirely to others; minimize your time in this quadrant.
- **Not urgent and not important:** Eliminate or postpone this work.

The following steps will help you learn more about the skills possessed by your team members and how to best delegate work:

1. Evaluate the skills and capacity of your team members. Some may have needed skills from previous employers that you aren't aware of. Document this in a skills inventory.

2. Consider developmental activities for each team member. You have a pretty good idea of this already as part of your one-on-one meetings (you are holding these, right?) and future work. Much of this will fall in the not urgent and not important category.

3. Identify tasks that are targets for delegation and the associated level of training that would be required to hand off the work.

4. Select team members who are candidates for delegation (skills, growth opportunities, capacity).

5. Put a plan in place to delegate the work.

Delegation is more than saying, "Here you go. You own this now." A good leader is intentional about delegation and ensuring that the work is transferred in an orderly fashion. Depending on the work to be delegated, the steps could be as simple as these:

1. You watch me do the work.
2. We do the work together.
3. I watch you perform the work.
4. You perform the work, and I review.
5. You own the work.

Tasks to consider delegating may include rotating status meeting updates to give everyone a chance to lead the meeting, asking different people to lead a book study, providing topics for research opportunities, documenting processes and procedures, or training new hires during onboarding. Keep in mind that it will likely take someone longer than a more experienced person in the beginning. Be patient. Most things are hard before they're easy.

Some things should never be delegated. These include things like goal and strategy setting, decision-making on critical issues, communicating key messages, leading organizational changes, and crisis management. And of course, things like one-on-one meetings, constructive feedback, team development, and performance reviews are your responsibility. This doesn't mean that you don't get input from others, but don't abdicate your responsibility.

Delegation is an important strategy in a leadership toolbox for developing team members, increasing productivity, and freeing you up to focus on higher-priority work.

## PRODUCTIVITY TIPS: THINGS TO STOP DOING

We've covered several tactics you can use to improve productivity: establishing morning or evening routines to help win the day, scheduling power sessions for focused work time, establishing office hours to answer questions, saying no to low-value work, and delegating work to team members to help them grow and develop while freeing up more of your time. Equally important is improving productivity by no longer doing things that are counterproductive:

- Stop multitasking. Now we know that no one can effectively do two cognitive tasks at the same time—it's really task switching and is inefficient.

- Stop checking social media throughout the day. Mindless scrolling through social media is a significant distraction. Take social media off your phone or check it only during breaks or outside work hours.

- Stop checking your phone constantly.

- Stop taking pictures of everything and posting them on social media, especially during work hours.

- Stop taking on other people's monkeys. Put the work back on them by saying, "I'm sure you'll be able to figure this out."

- Stop being busy being busy. Focus on high-value work, not on something that's fast, fun, and easy.

- Stop procrastinating. Delaying tasks only increases stress and decreases productivity. Use power blocks to tackle the delayed work.

- Stop letting people interrupt you. You can say, "I need to finish what I'm doing—can I follow up with you when I'm done?"

- Stop being a perfectionist. Strive for good enough and move on to the next task.

- Stop hanging around with people who bring you down.

- Stop allowing yourself to be manipulated. When some-one tries to guilt you into doing something, consider saying, "Let me think about that and get back to you." Set boundaries for yourself. Being nice doesn't mean being a doormat.

- Stop guessing what someone wants. Ask clarifying questions to avoid wasting time doing the wrong thing.

The tactics covered in this chapter are foundational to owning your day instead of your day owning you. The challenge is to replace old habits with new ones. You don't need to do everything in this chapter all at once. Pick one or two key tactics to focus on and turn those into habits. Each week or two, add to the list. If you don't have focused blocks of time scheduled, that's a great one to start with.

# CHAPTER ELEVEN

# IT'S ALL ABOUT ME— MEETING EFFECTIVENESS

**THE SVP OF QUALITY** in a large financial services company hired me as a project manager (PM) for part of a large quality assurance initiative for more than four thousand employees. It was during this engagement that I learned about how to run effective meetings. The initiative's program manager, Peter, scheduled thirty-minute weekly program status meetings with the twelve PMs to provide updates on each of our areas.

Before the first meeting, Peter scheduled an expectation-setting meeting with the PMs. He started the meeting by saying, "This is a fifty-five-million-dollar initiative that is sponsored by the company president. We have a lot to do and have brought in the resources needed for this to be successful. We will meet each week for thirty minutes. I will ask each of you the same questions: First, do you have a project schedule that the team has agreed to? If not, you'll be asked to leave the meeting and bring a schedule to next week's meeting. Second, are the tasks on schedule, yes or no? If yes, there are no more questions, and I'll move to the next PM. If the answer is no, do you need help to get it back on schedule? If yes, I'll ask where you need help, and you'll have one minute to summarize. We can schedule a follow-up meeting if it can't be addressed quickly. If you don't need help with corrective action, I will move to the next PM. I need truthful responses so that I can help you. Any questions?"

Most project status meetings I had attended in other companies had taken half an hour to cover one project. PMs usually talked about the work that had been accomplished, problems instead of solutions, and made excuses for why tasks were late. I must admit that I was skeptical that Peter was going to cover a dozen projects in half an hour.

Well, let me tell you that Peter ran the most effective and efficient meetings I've ever been in. The PMs were prepared, had taken initiative prior to the meeting to correct any issues, and were proactive on everything.

Peter was like the teacher who challenged you to be better than you thought you could be. He believed in every one of us and made us believe we could be successful. He set expectations, pitched in and helped out, and was always there to remove obstacles and resolve issues.

This initiative was delivered on time and within budget, and it became a benchmark in the industry for similar quality initiatives. Peter's team accomplished in eighteen months what other companies took five years to do. We had our share of problems, like any large program, but having an engaged, efficient, and competent program manager allowed the teams to take the needed corrective actions quickly and continue to make progress.

In that engagement, I learned a lot from Peter about how to do things the right way and about what is possible.

Unfortunately, this isn't the story that most of us hear when we talk about the meetings in our organizations. It's quite the opposite. Regardless of the sources of the many surveys and studies on meeting effectiveness, the results are the same: Most meetings are not productive, there are too many meetings, people are checking their phones / emails / chats, the wrong people are in the meetings, the people who do attend aren't well prepared or are not paying attention—the list goes on and on. Needless meetings interrupt the time required for knowledge work, and we've already established the negative effect of distractions on cognitive tasks.

Organizations have tight controls on budgets and finance but little to no controls on the *time* spent by the people in the organizations. Meeting invites are largely unchecked to see if the meeting is needed, if the right people are involved, if there's an agenda, and if the meeting even needs to be held. With an invitation being the click of a button in today's virtual world, it's easy to add someone just in case they may want to attend or if the meeting organizer believes that being collaborative means including anyone who may be interested in the topic.

The effective use of meetings provides a mechanism to improve productivity, keep projects on schedule, accelerate decision-making, develop plans, set priorities, discuss performance, review results, conduct interviews, share information, collaborate, innovate, and many other useful outcomes.

Most people say we have too many meetings. I believe the real issue is that we have too many ineffective meetings that waste people's time because we didn't properly prepare for them. If we lead effective and efficient meetings, perhaps we don't need as many.

Remember, people mimic the leader. It's up to you to set an example for effective meetings. What follows are fundamental tactics you can use to ensure productive meetings. Author

Samuel Jackson said, "People need to be reminded more than they need to be instructed." This is one of those topics. Most of us know what we should do to have a successful meeting, but we just don't do it. As a leader, set the right example.

## ALL MEETINGS ARE NOT CREATED EQUALLY

You wouldn't spend the same amount of time preparing for a weekly status meeting or a one-on-one with a team member as you would for presenting a business case to executives. Let's look at the most common meeting categories and how to prepare for and lead them.

Informational meetings include topics such as company news, policy changes, financial performance, upcoming initiatives, employee recognition, and safety and compliance findings. At the team level, an information meeting may be to cascade company information, give updates on specific work the team has done, share progress toward team goals, highlight recent wins and successes for the team, and provide an opportunity for people to ask questions. To prepare for an informational meeting, elicit input from team members, especially for recent wins and accomplishments, and keep track of the information you need to impart to your team on an ongoing basis. Set up a shared meeting template that you and team members can update to save time. You may also want to ask for questions in advance to have time to think about your answers. Informational meetings at the team level may be weekly, biweekly, or monthly.

Project meetings include kickoff meetings, status update meetings, and lessons learned. Project kickoff meetings impart information to project team members and stakeholders regarding the project's objectives, roles and responsibilities, milestones and timelines, and an overview of the workstreams. It's designed to get a common understanding up front and to set expectations about how the project will be managed.

Project status update meetings are regularly scheduled meetings to communicate project progress for the work planned against the schedule and budget, risks, issues, and areas where assistance is needed. At the project level, this is usually weekly but sometimes biweekly is sufficient. I've already given you suggestions for how to optimize these meetings by using Peter's example at the beginning of the chapter.

Lessons learned meetings are often held after a project has been completed, but at that point, it's a little late to take corrective action. I suggest conducting lessons learned meetings after key milestones are reached to see what is working well and what improvements must be made. No need to wait until the end of the project to make necessary changes.

Create a template for each of these types of project meetings for consistency and speed. If your company has a project management office, this team usually has a set of standard templates to use.

The third meeting category is problem-solving. These meetings include brainstorming sessions to generate creative ideas and solutions, troubleshooting meetings where a person or group brings a specific problem or challenge and works together to develop a solution, and conflict resolution meetings where individuals or groups work to resolve conflicts or disagreements. The meeting outcome is more important than an agenda in problem-solving meetings. The keys to successful problem-solving and decision-making meetings are to ensure that the problem or decision to be made is clearly defined and understood, the right people are in attendance, everyone gets a chance to share ideas and perspectives, and the meeting stays on point.

Every meeting should have specific outcomes, otherwise why have the meeting? Think about the type of meeting you are preparing for and apply the tactics appropriately. For example, my thirty-minute weekly status meetings have the same agenda: Are we on schedule and within budget? If not, why not? What are you doing to mitigate the overruns? What are the top risks and issues, and what are the mitigation strategies? What help do you need?

These categories of meetings have varying levels of complexity and require different levels of preparation and facilitation. The sections that follow are geared toward meetings that take more preparation and planning for the meeting facilitator and participants, such as problem-solving, decision-making, strategic planning and goal setting, or requirements-gathering meetings, to name a few.

## PREPARATION

Many of the meetings we attend aren't productive for any number of the reasons listed previously. Before you schedule a meeting, ask yourself two filtering questions: Is this meeting really necessary, or could I get the information through an email or add the topic to an existing meeting? Is this meeting needed now, or would it be beneficial to wait a few days when more information is available? Simply asking these two questions may reduce the number of meetings you schedule or attend.

If the meeting is needed, it's time to prepare for it by asking additional questions:

- Do I have all the information needed to make the meeting successful?
- Do I know how the meeting success will be measured?
- Are there areas for potential conflicts or tensions?
- Are there personality dynamics to take into consideration?

## MEETING AGENDAS

A well-thought-out agenda is the most important aspect of ensuring an effective meeting and is one of the most overlooked. How many times do you receive a calendar invitation without an agenda or even the purpose of the meeting? And how many times do you accept it? Effective leaders set the expectation that all meeting invitations have agendas. A participant in one of my leadership workshops had a great suggestion for this. He set up a rule in his email to auto-respond to all calendar invites: "I have received your calendar invite. If the invite includes an agenda, I'll review and accept it later today. However, if there isn't an agenda, please resend the invite with the agenda attached. This will help me prepare and make meaningful contributions to the meeting."

The agenda sets the expectations for the meeting (before and during), who should attend, what prep work is required in advance by the attendees, gets attendees aligned on the meeting topics, sets expectations for each topic (informational, input only needed, decision needed, actions), and the duration and location of the meeting.

**Topics.** Depending on the type of meeting being scheduled, seek input from meeting participants and others to collect the needed topics for discussion. Be specific about the topic.

Instead of listing a topic as "Budget Discussions," be explicit in what you expect. For example, at the end of the budget discussion, do you want approval? Permission to move forward? This helps the presenter understand what information is needed, the level of detail, and how it will be used. Remember the treadmill verbs from chapter 8 and be explicit.

**Attendees.** Only invite the people who are needed to the meeting. This bears repeating—send the meeting notice only to the people who need to attend. Too many people tend to derail the meeting. If someone's presence isn't really necessary, they are disengaged and probably texting others on how boring this meeting is. Leave them off the invite.

Not everyone who must be informed has to be at the meeting—keep that in mind when you begin to change who you invite. You can provide an update after the meeting to those who need to be included.

The flip side is to ensure that you have everyone who is required so that you don't have to reschedule the meeting later. If some of the participants aren't necessary for all topics, have them participate when needed and excuse them once their part is done.

One of my pet peeves is when I send a meeting invite to a selected group of attendees and the invite is forwarded to more people, usually without asking. If I am intentional about the attendees, I will add a note to the invite that says not to forward it without permission and that includes a good reason. When an attendee forwards the invite, I ask them to let me know if they both need to attend and specifically why the additional person is needed.

**Timing for Topics.** Some meetings are more formal than others. Meetings that need to stay on track should have time slots for each topic as well as who is responsible for leading the discussion. This helps keep the dialogue focused and minimizes tangents. Think through how much time each topic may need and where more or less time may be required. Will the owner of the topic need to provide background information? Will there be questions? Is a decision required? If so, how much time might that take?

**Meeting Duration.** Some meetings require more time than others. What meetings do you have that don't really need an hour? Could they be done in half an hour? Forty-five minutes? Shorter meetings tend to keep people more focused, and they come better prepared. Are there other ways to cover the information faster and more efficiently? For example, do you know the key milestones for each project the team member is working on? If so, the meeting can be a quick and simple conversation, as follows:

1. Are the tasks on schedule?
2. If not, what is the mitigation plan, and what are the impacts?
3. What help do you need from me?

Or you may ask for a weekly status update so that the information can be quickly consumed. If everything is on schedule, there is no need to have a meeting to report that. Remember the first filtering question: Is this meeting really needed? Could I get the needed information through an email or add the topic to an existing meeting?

**Required Prep.** Meeting participants need to know what preparation is required prior to the meeting, and the information should be provided in advance to allow time to review. Put links to the documents in the meeting invite for ease of use. If there are several references, it may also be helpful to include a description and why it's important to the meeting.

No one likes to receive supporting documentation the night before or during the meeting without sufficient time to review it. If we truly value others' time, send information in advance with time to review and ask questions.

**Expectations.** The calendar invite and meeting agenda set the expectations for the meeting.

- The meeting will start promptly at 8:00 a.m. We have a lot to cover. Please make every effort to be on time.

- Complete the prep work in advance so that you are prepared for the discussions and decision-making.

- This is an important meeting. Please turn off cell phones and close your email until after the meeting.

- We are not here to focus on the past but to decide on the best solutions moving forward.

## MEETING SUCCESS

The CEO of a client company asked me to facilitate their annual strategic planning session. I agreed and asked, "How would you finish this sentence: This meeting will be successful if . . ."

He looked at me and said, "That's a good question. I'll need to think about that."

Prior to the strategic planning meeting, I sent an email to each person on the executive team, asking them to complete the same sentence. The responses had common elements but different topics they wanted to address. During a weekly executive staff meeting, we reviewed the purpose and success criteria for the upcoming meeting and gained alignment on what would be included and how we would determine whether the meeting was successful. Asking this one simple question made a big difference in how we all prepared for the off-site.

As the leader, define the success criteria for your meetings and ensure that every meeting participant knows what this is. This tends to help keep the meeting on track.

The need to define success is different for various types of meetings. For example, success for a one-on-one meeting with a team member may be to have actionable steps that the team member can take to move their growth forward with a time frame for completion. Success criteria for a two-day strategic planning meeting may include a clearly defined direction for the organization for the next six months, goals and objectives, a road map for execution, and an approved budget to support the road map.

## MEETING FACILITATION

Running effective meetings takes a lot of concentration and management. For highly critical or contentious meetings, it may be prudent to hire a facilitator who is trained in how to mitigate difficult situations and help people reach decisions. Most of the time, however, our meetings don't fall into this category, and the use of a trained facilitator is either not required or not an option, leaving it to the leader to play the facilitator role of ensuring that the meeting stays on track.

Start the meeting on time. Welcome attendees and thank them for being there. Remind everyone to turn off their cell phones and pay attention, and request participation from everyone. If the meeting is one of high importance, have a senior executive kick it off to help set the right tone for the remainder of the topics. Repeat the meeting's purpose. This is also a good time to complete the sentence: "This meeting will be successful if . . ." to remind participants of the meeting's end goal.

It's distracting and rude when people arrive late to a meeting and then further interrupt by apologizing or explaining why they were late. "I'm so sorry I'm late. Traffic was brutal. There was an accident on the freeway, and I was late dropping my kid off at school." If you're late, everyone already knows it and probably doesn't care about the reason. Brian Tracy, motivational speaker, said, "If you're not early, you're late." Punctuality reflects a commitment to professionalism and respect for others' time.

If someone joins five or ten minutes late, don't spend the next five minutes catching them up. When you do, you disrespect everyone who showed up on time and send a message that being late doesn't really matter.

Assign someone to take meeting notes and capture action items for future follow-up. The action items should include the person responsible for resolution, a due date, and how the resolution will be communicated to the team.

Keep the meeting on schedule. Don't let people ramble or talk longer than necessary. If something comes up that requires more discussion, capture it in the meeting notes and follow up later. Some people like to hear themselves talk and will dominate the conversation if allowed. Remind them of the time constraints and the need to hear from all participants.

## MEETING WRAP-UP

Do your meetings stop or end? When I worked in Washington, DC, it was common for meeting participants to look at the clock, interrupt the person talking, and say something like, "I have to go now. My metro train leaves in ten minutes." Then they would gather their belongings and walk out of the room.

I learned the metro schedule quickly and held meetings earlier in the day to avoid the abrupt endings. Leave time at the end of meetings to summarize the highlights and to discuss action items and next steps.

## MEETING +/-

At times, it's helpful to take the pulse on the quality of your meetings. Periodically, save a few minutes at the end of the meeting to ask the participants what went well and what could be improved. Everyone learns from this exercise and can use the information for when they are leading their own meetings. Areas to consider include the following:

1. Was the purpose of the meeting clearly understood?
2. Did the meeting outcomes satisfy the success criteria?
3. How well prepared were the participants?
4. Was the needed information provided with sufficient time for review?
5. Was there additional information that would've been helpful?
6. Were the meeting participants engaged?

7. Was the amount of time for the meeting topics appropriate?
8. Is everyone aware of the action items they own?
9. What could've been done better?

Remember, people mimic the leader. When others see you preparing for a meeting, starting the meeting on time, turning off your cell phone, setting clear expectations, defining meeting success, leading a successful meeting, asking for updates on outstanding action items, and asking for feedback, they will start to do the same.

## CHAPTER TWELVE

# PUT SYSTEMS IN PLACE

---

**YOU'VE LIKELY READ THE STORY** of the man cutting down a tree with a dull axe. Another guy walks by and says, "If you'd sharpen the axe, you could cut that tree down a lot faster." The first guy says, "I don't have time." If you set aside focused time to think about the task at hand, you may decide that a chain saw is an even better solution!

Steve was designated as the person to train new employees coming into his department. For every new hire, he scheduled multiple video calls to walk each of them through the software systems they would be using and to explain the role. About 25 percent of his time was spent ramping up new hires. I asked, "Why do you spend so much time training each person individually?"

"The information is all in my head."

I asked, "Would documenting it make it easier?"

"Yes, of course, but I don't have time."

"Can you record the virtual meetings while you're training someone and use those videos for future training?" I asked.

I saw the light bulb go off in his head. "Yes, that's a great idea." (The chain saw)

What opportunities do you and your team have to streamline, document, and automate workflows and processes?

## SYSTEMS MAKE LIFE EASIER

James Clear, author of *Atomic Habits*, writes, "You do not rise to the level of your goals. You fall to the level of your systems."[10] Why not take the time to put systems in place for the routine work that you do? Like Steve, most people say they don't have time. What we find is that when we never have the time to do it right, we seem to find the time to do it over (and over).

This also applies to just about everything. When we don't define the problem clearly, we waste people's time in meetings and solve the wrong problems. When we don't take the time to understand a client's requirements, we build the wrong thing and lose credibility. When we don't automate processes and workflows, we waste time, are inconsistent, and cost the company money. That's why good leaders like you build systems for themselves and their team members.

Systems aren't just software for project planning, time management, accounting and finance, human resources, inventory management, or supply chain management. Systems also include templates for documents (e.g., status reporting, meeting agendas, action items, project documentation, emails, forms, and many others); processes to capture how workflows are performed; RACI charts for who does what; knowledge repositories so that you know where to find things; policies that govern how things are to be done; and standards and guidelines to maintain consistency across an organization.

Imagine that you have a weekend project to build a tree house, and the plans call for you to cut fifty two-by-four boards to the same length. You could measure each board to the same length, one board at a time, and cut each board individually. Or you could build a jig (think: system) to save time and ensure accuracy. You'd line the boards up in the jig, measure to the desired length, and cut several at the same time, each exactly the same length and with little to no thinking required.

You want to do the same thing at work. When you document a workflow or define a process, you solve the problem or issue once. For example, if a document requires review and approval from several people, define that once. If it can be automated using an e-signature, that's even better. Then, no one has to think about who needs to review and approve the document.

Assign a process owner. Anytime you can reduce the number of handoffs within a process, the better. For example, assigning a person (or a group of people) to own onboarding new employees from offer acceptance to start date and orientation results in a much better new-hire experience and fewer opportunities for things to fall through the cracks (like the computer failing to arrive by the start date). One person responsible for a work stream makes it much easier to measure performance and mitigates finger-pointing.

Look for ways to systematize as much as possible for quality, consistency, accuracy, and speed. It's not a good use of time to be thinking about how the monthly report should be formatted—the usefulness of the content is much more important than the right font. Develop a template so that the focus is on content, organized in the most optimal way.

Steve's story about training every person individually is another example of where automation and consistency are important. Using videos to train new hires as part of the onboarding process not only provides consistency and higher quality but also allows the employee to refer to training as often as needed. If changes are made, it's much easier to communicate the changes to employees and ask them to watch the revised training videos than to retrain them all in person. Systems make our lives easier.

## WHY DON'T WE PUT MORE SYSTEMS IN PLACE?

In my consulting work in more than twenty companies, I see opportunities for systems (or improved systems) in almost all areas. If systems make our lives easier, why don't we put more of them, and better ones, in place?

As mentioned earlier, this takes time. Some systems take more time than others and may require a budget that hasn't been planned for. You are likely aware of areas where taking a few hours to define or document a process or to develop a template would save a lot of time, confusion, and errors.

One client company had a software release problem that was easily solved by organizing and sharing a calendar with assigned release dates to different departments. In another, it took a few hours to document and communicate a checklist for salespeople to use when submitting a loan application for processing. If you look carefully at the work that you and your team are responsible for, my bet is that you have several opportunities to systematize an area that has caused friction. If you're working on your set-my-day-up-for-success routine, you'll have time to make the needed improvements when you use the uninterrupted blocks of time for focused thinking.

Some people believe that if it ain't broke, don't fix it. That may be OK in some cases, but this attitude is problematic if the process works but it's slow or inefficient, like Steve's individual training for new hires instead of recording it.

Maybe you aren't aware that a change is warranted. Once

you start looking for things to systematize, your reticular activating system (RAS) that we learned about earlier will bring these opportunities into clear focus. You'll start to become aware of more areas that benefit from improvements or that need a system. You can also ask your team members for ideas. They are often the closest to the problem and have thoughts on how to improve workflows.

Sometimes I've gotten pushback when introducing a process or template. I hear things like this: "You're stifling my creativity," "You're creating too much overhead," and "Do you want me to fill out this template or get my work done?" Obviously, we don't want to create a process or a system that isn't helpful or needed. Clearly communicate the problem you want to solve and why it's important (multiple times). Ask team members for their input to help get buy-in. Then train everyone on the process or template to alleviate fears or concerns.

Two of my favorite systems are targeted at problem-solving and decision-making, and both are critical skills a leader should have.

## A PROBLEM-SOLVING SYSTEM: USING CAUSE-AND-EFFECT DIAGRAMS

As a leader, you will undoubtedly spend a fair amount of time anticipating and solving problems. Some problems have simple solutions while others require more in-depth analysis. It's possible to misidentify a problem, thinking it's one thing when it's actually just a symptom of a larger issue. To help us better understand and solve problems, we have a tool called the cause-and-effect diagram.

The cause-and-effect diagram was created by Dr. Kaoru Ishikawa in the 1960s to help improve quality control processes in shipbuilding. You may know it as the fishbone diagram or the Ishikawa diagram. This tool helps us visually see the possible causes of a problem we want to solve. It also helps us organize related issues into categories to define the problem better.

To use this tool, we first need to know the meanings of the words *cause* and *effect*. The cause is the reason why something happened. For example, if you get a speeding ticket, the cause is that you were driving above the speed limit, and a police officer happened to measure your speed with a radar gun. The effect is what happened, which, in this case, is getting a speeding ticket.

A problem can have multiple causes, meaning there could be several reasons for a particular effect or issue. The cause-and-effect diagram helps us to identify these causes systematically. By doing so, we can focus our efforts on addressing the root cause(s) of a problem rather than just the symptoms.

The graphic that follows shows an example of low employee engagement (the effect) with multiple causes contributing to the problem.

Let's go through the steps that were followed to create this diagram.

**Step 1: Define the Problem.** Defining a problem might seem easy at first, but it can be more complicated than it appears. Sometimes we rely too much on our past experiences and jump to conclusions, thinking we know what the problem is. However, this can lead to misidentifying the problem and only treating its symptoms. For example, someone may say that there are too many application errors, but that could be just one factor contributing to the larger issue of poor product quality.

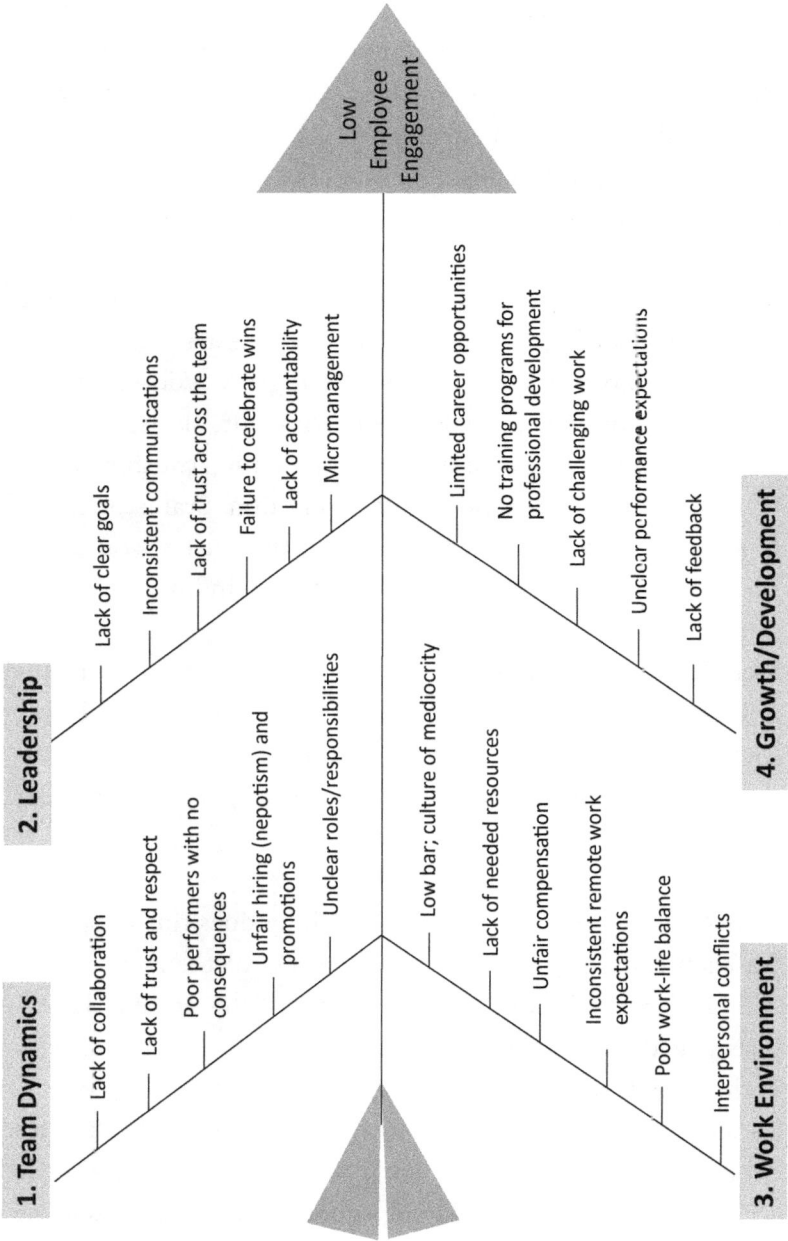

Low Employee Engagement

**2. Leadership**
- Lack of clear goals
- Inconsistent communications
- Lack of trust across the team
- Failure to celebrate wins
- Lack of accountability
- Micromanagement

**4. Growth/Development**
- Limited career opportunities
- No training programs for professional development
- Lack of challenging work
- Unclear performance expectations
- Lack of feedback

**1. Team Dynamics**
- Lack of collaboration
- Lack of trust and respect
- Poor performers with no consequences
- Unfair hiring (nepotism) and promotions
- Unclear roles/responsibilities

**3. Work Environment**
- Low bar; culture of mediocrity
- Lack of needed resources
- Unfair compensation
- Inconsistent remote work expectations
- Poor work-life balance
- Interpersonal conflicts

To develop an accurate problem statement, take the time to identify the real problem, not just the contributing factors. Defining the problem accurately is crucial to finding the root cause and addressing it effectively.

The problem statement becomes the head of the fishbone diagram. In our diagram, this is low employee engagement.

**Step 2: Develop the Cause Categories.** The categories of the cause of the problem in the previous example are team dynamics, leadership, work environment, and growth/development. Other categories may include environment, skills, external forces, equipment, and control. For marketing, categories may include product, place, price, and promotion. Brainstorm four to six categories under which most of the causes would fall. List the categories as branches from the main line.

**Step 3: Document Possible Causes.** Brainstorm the various possible causes that contribute to the problem statement, listing each of them under the appropriate category(s). In some cases, one cause may fall under more than one category—list it under all that apply.

**Step 4: Ask Why.** Continue to ask "Why does this happen?" for each cause to continue drilling down to the root causes. This technique is called the five whys. Why are employees disengaged? Because there is high turnover on the team. Why is there high turnover on the team? Because employees feel undervalued. Why do employees feel undervalued? Because they aren't recognized for their work. Why is there little recognition? Because leadership doesn't prioritize employee recognition. Why doesn't the organization prioritize employee recognition? Because leadership focuses only on financial metrics, not on employee morale.

**Step 5: Analyze the Causes.** After listing all the possible causes, it's time to analyze the diagram as a group. Look for patterns and causes that appear more than once. You'll probably notice several common themes that come up. This is an important part of the exercise because identifying these patterns can help pinpoint the root cause of the problem. In our example, several causes are related to the lack of trust and clarity.

**Step 6: Prioritize.** Now that you've analyzed the diagram to identify the root cause of the problem, it's time to prioritize how to address the issues. Look at the diagram and figure out which areas can be fixed easily to take advantage of low-hanging fruit. Also, consider which causes have the biggest impact on the problem. By doing this, you can determine which issues need to be tackled first and which ones can wait. This helps you make the most effective use of your time and resources to address the problem.

Based on this example, which would you prioritize?

If you want to improve your problem-solving skills and become a more effective leader, add the cause-and-effect diagram to your leadership toolbox. This powerful strategy is often overlooked in many companies, but it can help you tackle even the most complex problems. By visually representing the causes of a problem, you can identify the root cause and develop a plan of action to address it.

## DECISION-MAKING SYSTEMS

Decision-making is a critical part of a leader's role, and its importance cannot be overstated. The higher up you are, the harder the decisions are. Remember, leaders don't get the easy stuff. You must make informed (based on the available information) and timely decisions to guide your teams to success. Some decisions are relatively easy to make, such as implementing a morning routine, investing in personal growth, or always being honest. Other decisions (e.g., What should we do about having people come back into the office after a pandemic?) are more complex and require a more detailed decision-making process.

In your leadership role, you have many types of decisions to deal with on a regular basis that affect the health and well-being of people, teams, and the company. You decide the department's vision—how to prioritize the highest-value work while balancing budgets and resources. You decide the best mitigation strategies when assessing risks and issues and the corrective actions to take when things don't go as planned. You decide which candidate to hire based on the job requirements you decided were the most important. You decide which team member to promote, what training is appropriate for personal growth, and the consequences for low performers. You make decisions on how to best resolve conflicts. Decision fatigue is real and consumes a lot of energy.

## FILTERING FOR DECISION-MAKING

Like most things, not all decisions are created equally. Let's look at filtering as a tactic to make our decision-making life easier. Deciding what to wear to work each day is probably not too challenging for most of us. We consider things like the weather, the season, the meetings we need to attend, and what's clean. Steve Jobs, former Apple CEO, simplified the decision-making process even more by wearing his signature black turtleneck shirt, beltless jeans, and running shoes every day. No decision required. We can do the same thing by setting up filters for our personal and professional lives.

In the book *10X Is Easier Than 2X*, authors Dan Sullivan and Dr. Benjamin Hardy share a filter used by the British Olympic rowing team.[11] Each member of the team asked, "Will this make the boat go faster?" for all decisions, including social activities, nutrition, training, or rest. Will going to a party and staying up late make the boat go faster? Hmm, probably not. Will eating this kind of food make the boat go faster? Will streamlining communications during training and races make the boat go faster?

You can set similar filters with questions such as these:

- Is this the highest-value work I should be doing right now?
- Is this aligned with my core values?
- Is this aligned with my team's goals?
- Will this make me more productive?
- Will this help build trust with my team?
- Will this advance my career?

If the answer is yes, do whatever it is. If the answer is no, don't.

Will implementing a morning routine make me more productive? Yes, absolutely. I'll put a routine in place.

Will attending meetings that don't have an agenda or a purpose make me more productive? No, it will waste my time. I'll require an agenda or decline the meeting.

Filters eliminate agonizing about what you should do and simplify the decision-making process. It's a simple yes or no response.

## A SEVEN-STEP DECISION-MAKING PROCESS

Sometimes we need to make decisions that aren't so cut and dry, with multiple alternatives. For these types of decisions, a more robust process is helpful. Examples include selecting vendors to implement solutions, deciding on a company location, and determining the best strategies for increasing revenues and lowering costs, to name a few. In these types of examples, a process helps guide us to a better decision.

Let's look at a seven-step process to help you assess the situation, gather information, consider alternatives, and make a choice that best aligns with the team or organization.

**Step 1: Identify the Decision Needed.** This seems painfully obvious, but often it's not. For example, Martin, an executive in one of my client companies, asked me to teach a course on estimating project schedules and resources because most all their projects were late and over budget. I told him that I could do that, but before we went down that path, I asked him to send me the requirements documents that the project manager and team members were using that described the work to be done. Some projects didn't have requirements defined at all and most other requirements documents were unclear and incomplete. I explained to Martin that this was like asking a home builder to build you a house in the suburbs and wanting to know the cost and how long it would take. Teaching project teams how to estimate was solving the wrong problem. They needed to learn how to gather and document requirements first. You can use the cause-and-effect diagram discussed in the previous section to dissect the problem to gain insights into what decision is needed.

Don't make a decision that solves the wrong problem.

**Step 2: Gather Relevant Information**. Often we simply don't dedicate sufficient time and energy to make critical decisions, or we rush to say, "I know what we should do." In the 1960s, when NASA started to send astronauts into space, they found that ballpoint pens wouldn't work in zero-gravity conditions. A private company spent over a million dollars and about a decade to develop pressurized ink cartridges, overcomplicating the issue. Meanwhile, the Russians used pencils.

Gather the information needed and break down the problem into manageable chunks. List potential risks and issues that the problem creates. Meet with stakeholders to get their perspectives and understand their needs.

**Step 3: Identify Alternatives**. Several techniques are available to determine potential solutions. First, set up filters to quickly eliminate alternatives that don't match your criteria. For example, if you're looking for a new office location, you may have a filter of "within one mile of public transportation." Anything outside that distance is not considered, and you save a lot of time by removing it from the analysis step.

An internet search will likely provide several solutions to pursue. Additionally, brainstorming may help generate more ideas and alternatives. You can also reach out to other companies and learn which alternatives they considered and the one selected. It's helpful to visit other companies to see how they have solved similar problems and the decisions they made.

**Step 4: Analyze Alternatives.** The information generated in the first three steps prepares the team for analyzing each alternative. Consider each alternative in terms of feasibility, cost-benefit, time and cost to implement, ease of implementation, staffing and skills needs, impact to stakeholders, and risks.

**Step 5: Select the Solution.** At this point, you have a good understanding of the alternatives, along with the pros and cons of each. Select the best solution based on the completed analysis.

**Step 6: Measure Twice, Cut Once.** Now that a decision has been reached, step back and take a hard look before starting to implement it. It's tempting and easy to fall in love with a choice or to be relieved that one has been made. Review the decision with stakeholders who weren't involved in the process to get feedback on potential flaws, possible risks, or blind spots that may have been overlooked.

**Step 7: Take Action.** After the decision has been made, communicate it to the stakeholders and start to work. Plan out the work, execute, report the results, and course-correct as needed.

This chapter gives you several ideas for where you can put systems in place that will save you and your team time, scale your efforts, and improve consistency. Sometimes these are tasks that make good developmental opportunities for team members.

This section on productivity habits covers a lot of tactics and techniques for setting your day up for success with routines, focused blocks of time, delegation, saying no to low-value work, running effective meetings, and putting systems in place.

The good news is that you don't need to put everything into practice immediately. Pick two or three tactics that resonated with you and work on those first. You can add more later. For example, could you start by adding agendas to all your meeting invitations if you aren't already doing this? Could you ask meeting organizers to send you an agenda when it's missing? Could you schedule a one-hour block once or twice a week for focused time? Could you get up fifteen minutes earlier for thinking time? Could you find one thing to delegate to a team member?

Remember that it's the little things that make the most difference over time.

**Awareness**

**Effective Communication**

**High-Performing Teams**

**Lead by Example**

**Productivity Habits**

**Exceptional Results**

# PART FIVE

# EXCEPTIONAL RESULTS

A goal without a plan is just a wish.

**—ANTOINE DE SAINT-EXUPÉRY**

**LEADERSHIP IS ULTIMATELY MEASURED** by the results and outcomes you achieve. Individual contributors are usually assigned work, and success is determined by skills, hard work, and the ability to deliver. But as a leader, your success is about what you can accomplish through others.

Your skills must include the ability to set clear, impactful goals, prioritize them effectively, and develop actionable plans so that everyone is working together, moving in the same direction. Without knowing the highest-value work, time is wasted by people working on the wrong things that don't move the needle in the right direction. Busy being busy doesn't always mean productive. Leadership is about doing the right things, not just doing things. Let's look at how to use goal setting to ensure that you understand the highest-value work for prioritizing and planning.

# CHAPTER THIRTEEN

# ESTABLISH GOALS TO REMOVE SILOS AND FRICTION

**LEADERS IN MOST COMPANIES** don't do a great job at goal setting, even though they might argue otherwise. Let's be honest. Most companies miss the mark when it comes to goal setting. What do companies keep getting wrong? One of the most common things I see is setting goals in silos, if at all. Let me give you an example.

I am genetically wired to organize, prioritize, and execute. This served me well when I moved into my first role of building and leading a project management office that prioritized, managed, and reported on all the projects in the company. I quickly realized the inefficiencies caused by siloed goal setting. Communications across departments were lacking, and executives were blindsided when scarce resources were needed from their teams. They were frustrated when things were implemented that didn't meet their needs and that required rework. Few projects were delivered on time because of missed requirements from other departments. Budget overruns were common with the rework and changes in the scope of work. Work was unorganized, and leaders lamented that their days were mostly reactive, feeling like little was accomplished at the end of the day.

I had my work cut out for me to figure out how to support organizational goals by bundling up all the related departmental work streams into one cohesive project to orchestrate work in a unified fashion. From my PMO vantage point, the need for cross-functional collaboration for goal setting became obvious. This is no small undertaking in most organizations, requiring executive support and a lot of effort. However, the payoff is huge.

Maybe you think it's not important to write down goals or to constantly remind others of them. Think again. When you're leading a cross-functional team of people to achieve company goals, it's important that everyone is on the same page. New people may come onto the team. Write your goals down, then remind people of them on a regular basis and why each goal is important. Otherwise, no one is communicating, and the results are subpar. In your leadership role, look for goals where work should be aggregated into a coordinated effort so that everyone who has an interest in or will be affected by the work is on the same page with the same priorities.

Imagine moving from a reactive whack-a-mole day, wondering what surprises will derail your plans, to one where you and your team know the top three things you need to get done for the day or week and are able to complete planned work. You go home at the end of the workday feeling like you've accomplished something and know what you'll be working on tomorrow. You enjoy dinner with your spouse and kids and leave the work stress behind. Properly setting goals helps make this a reality.

I know that work isn't always this predictable and that

things pop up unexpectedly. However, when you use the tools from previous chapters in conjunction with goal setting, you'll be better equipped to handle the curveballs that are thrown your way.

Let's move on to another benefit of setting goals.

## USE GOALS TO INCREASE PRODUCTIVITY

Most every leader believes that setting goals is a good idea, especially for other teams. It seems that we tend to think we're special and that things don't apply to us. "That's a great idea for you, but luckily, I don't need to do it. It doesn't apply to me. My team already knows what to do [fill in the blank]." Suspend the belief that you are special, if you feel that way, and agree to formalize your goals. When you do this, you lay the foundation to gain the clarity needed to prioritize work for your team. Everyone knows what is expected and what they should be working on. Goals eliminate confusion and increase productivity and morale. Employees have a sense of accomplishment and can be proud of their achievements.

Goals are measurable, and progress toward meeting them can be tracked. This helps build momentum and keeps the team motivated until the goal is reached. It also makes it easier to set expectations, determine whether a course correction is needed, and provide feedback for performance reviews.

When your goals are aligned with the organization and with department or division goals, resource management, decision-making, and communications are much easier.

## GOAL-SETTING TRAPS

With all the benefits of goal setting, why do so many companies do it so poorly? Let's look at several reasons.

## SEMANTICS ARE CONFUSING

Some people believe that a task or a project is a goal. For example, a sales leader may say they have a goal to hire ten more salespeople. That's just a task that might need to be done in support of a goal to increase revenue. Or an HR leader says she's going to implement a performance review system. That's a project supporting a goal to improve engagement and accountability.

When developing the goal-setting part of my leadership workshop, I spent the better part of several days sorting through the various definitions for goals, objectives, strategies, projects, actions, tasks, milestones, and measures. It was one of the most confusing exercises I've been through. Because consistent definitions don't seem to exist, what follows is how I apply the terms and definitions in a framework that I have used for years as a leader and with my clients. If you like other terms, by all means, use those. These have worked for me for years and have helped several clients improve their goal-setting process.

A *goal* is the outcome you want to achieve. For example, for-profit organizations usually have a goal to increase revenue and profit by some percentage for the year. A nonprofit may have a goal to increase the number of donors by some percentage.

A *strategy* is an approach taken to achieve a goal. A strategy to increase revenue may be to grow by acquiring companies. Another may be to introduce new products or services to increase the number of customers. Examples of common strategies to increase profitability include improving operational efficiencies using automation and artificial intelligence, restructuring the organization to eliminate redundancies, or using outsourcing companies to perform work less expensively.

An *action plan* comprises the specific actions that will be taken to deliver on the strategies. Often these are projects. For example, if a company decided to implement a new CRM solution in support of a goal to improve customer relationships, this is a large project that likely involves multiple departments and that requires a sizeable budget.

On a smaller scale, an action plan may be something like documenting a process from end to end for a better understanding of how things work. This may be one or more tasks, but unless it's a complex process, it probably doesn't warrant being a project.

A *measure* is how we determine whether the goal has been achieved. Measures must be quantifiable and specific so that there is no ambiguity of progress toward a goal. For example, it's usually easy to determine measures for revenue, profit margin, operating expense ratio, and voluntary attrition. Surveys can be used to measure things like employee engagement, employee satisfaction, and customer satisfaction.

## GOALS AREN'T WRITTEN DOWN OR COMMUNICATED

Too often, individual goals aren't written down or communicated to leaders and teams in a way that allows them to understand how their work contributes to departmental or organizational goals. In my workshops, I ask participants what their department goals are. Usually, the response is a blank stare. Many have not seen anything written down. They go about their day working on things they think are important. After one workshop, I followed up with the division leader of this client, a C-suite executive, who responded, "No, we didn't write them down, but everyone should know what they should be doing." I hear this a lot: "They should know what to do."

Why would an executive think their leaders should know the most important things to be working on when they don't know what the division goals are, the problems the executive is dealing with, or how the executive is being measured? As a leader, don't assume that your team members should somehow know what they should be working on. Be clear on team and individual goals.

Your manager probably will not hand you a document with perfectly written department goals. Most likely, you'll need to gain an understanding of their goals so that you have somewhere to start from when planning your own goals. Get confirmation that your proposed goals are aligned to the next level. Don't leave this to chance.

Maybe you're concerned about asking your manager or executive what their goals are. Will they think that you should already know this? Will they think that you don't know how to do your job? I understand your concern. Refer to chapter 8, where I talk about the importance of getting clarifications early on rather than waiting and working on the wrong things. You could say something like this: "I think I have a pretty good idea of what your goals are, but I want to be sure that we're on the same page so that I don't waste your time later. I believe that your goals are to [insert here]. Is this correct, or do we need to fine-tune them?" If you're unsure about the goals, you could say, "I need to have clarity on your goals so that I align mine to yours. I want to be efficient when working on my goals and help you achieve yours." What manager doesn't want to have efficient people working to help them meet their goals? It's much better to ask for goal clarity up front than to guess incorrectly and waste time on the wrong things.

## TOO MANY GOALS

One of my clients proudly reported that the executive team had developed more than one hundred goals during their off-site strategic planning session. When I reviewed the list, most of them were projects or tasks. We reviewed the definitions for each term in the framework and went back to the basics of what the goals were. Then we grouped the related items from the list and created projects. The amount of work was almost three times the annual budget! This resulted in a prioritization meeting where the highest-value projects were selected that could realistically be achieved with the resources and budget.

As a rule of thumb, three to five goals are manageable. As a reminder, a goal is something like this: Improve customer satisfaction from 92 percent to 96 percent by year's end. It's not this: Send out a customer satisfaction survey. The latter is a task that needs to be completed to help achieve the goal. If you state your goal properly, you can see how more than a few goals could dilute focus. If you reach a goal early, you can always add a new one.

## FEAR OF FAILURE

Thomas, the sales VP at a client company, shared his sales projections with me in advance of the annual off-site planning meeting. His goal was to increase sales by 3 percent by the end of the year. When I questioned him on such a low goal when competitors were growing at a rate more than double this, Thomas replied, "I want to be sure I can hit it because my bonus is tied to it." His bonus was more important to him than ensuring that the company was competitive.

Sometimes you may be concerned about setting a goal too high. What happens if you miss it? Will your bonus be affected? Will your performance review take a hit? Will you lose credibility with your manager? Will your team blame you? I understand the concerns.

If you target goals that are too low, complacency starts to set in. Innovative and creative ways of thinking are stifled. The team can hit the goal by exerting a little more effort or by manipulating numbers. But that doesn't help the company be competitive or innovative. It just keeps people in their comfort zone.

## Framework for Goals, Strategies, Actions, Measures

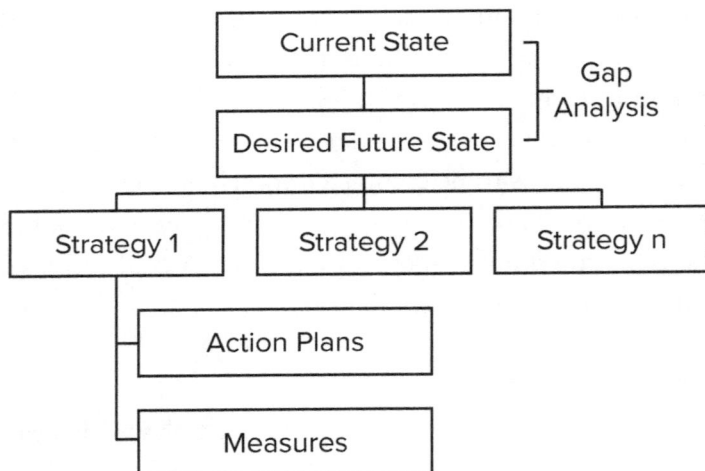

```
           ┌─────────────────────┐
           │    Current State    │──┐
           └─────────────────────┘  │  Gap
           ┌─────────────────────┐  │ Analysis
           │ Desired Future State│──┘
           └─────────────────────┘

┌──────────────┐  ┌──────────────┐  ┌──────────────┐
│  Strategy 1  │  │  Strategy 2  │  │  Strategy n  │
└──────────────┘  └──────────────┘  └──────────────┘

      ┌──────────────────┐
      │   Action Plans   │
      └──────────────────┘
      ┌──────────────────┐
      │     Measures     │
      └──────────────────┘
```

Focus on the top three things that your team could do that would add the most value. Do you need to streamline processes? Implement new tools to enhance productivity? Reorganize a department to be more efficient? Develop a new product? This is the type of thinking you want to do as part of your focused blocks of time. This one step starts to build the foundation for concentrating on the most important work. It doesn't need to be perfect. Just start with the top three things you believe are the most important. They may change over time when more information is available. You'll get better with practice.

## A GOAL-SETTING FRAMEWORK

You already know that I love systems, so it's no surprise that I have a framework to guide you through a strategic planning exercise. It's based on a current state/future state model as shown next.

Let's look at each component in the framework.

## CURRENT STATE

The current state defines where you are today in specific areas. For example, what are the current annual revenue, profit margins, operating expenses, cycle times, client satisfaction rating, market share, new product revenue, voluntary employee attrition, trouble ticket resolution time, or cost of compliance violations? This is your starting point in the framework. Establish a baseline of the measures that are important in your area of responsibility.

If you don't have a baseline measure, you'll want to establish one to track progress against it. Don't overcomplicate it. Earlier in my career, I built several project management offices for client companies. The current state when I started resembled chaos—little project documentation, lack of project management skills, schedule overruns, and client complaints.

I began by conducting project assessments to get an understanding of how projects were approved, initiated, documented, and managed, scoring each of them across project management best practices. I captured information on the number of current projects, how many resources were assigned to each one, whether the projects were on schedule, how many people worked on more than one, which ones had business cases, if there were standard project deliverables, how the deliverables were reviewed and approved, who the executive sponsor was and their commitment, and where project documentation was stored. I also interviewed project managers, clients, and managers to get their perspectives. This defined the current state and initial baseline. It took about a week to complete and provided a great snapshot of the current state of the company's projects and where I'd need to focus my efforts.

You may have to do something similar in your area of responsibility. Assessments, surveys, or interviews can provide the necessary insights quickly.

## DESIRED FUTURE STATE

Many companies hold annual planning sessions in which they strategize for the company's future. Future state in this context is what you want to accomplish at the end of the year (or by some specified time). This sets the direction so that leaders and their teams know what the year-end goals are. We'll talk more about how to plan the work in smaller increments of time in the next chapter.

As mentioned earlier, some leaders may have a desired future state that is more of the same or slightly better (especially if their bonus is tied to it), afraid that they will fail if they set the goal too high. Although this is understandable, it doesn't encourage innovation or lead to a competitive advantage.

Remember the large quality assurance program Peter led in the previous chapter? We were able to complete the program and achieve the expected business value in eighteen months when it took other companies five years. Had Peter settled for industry benchmarks, the program would've been planned for five years instead of a year and a half.

I invite you to think like great leaders think. Michelangelo, artist and sculptor, shared his perspective in this quote: "The greatest danger for most of us lies not in setting our aim too high and falling short but in setting our aim too low and achieving our mark."

You can use several approaches to help define what a realistic future state should be. As an example, look for companies that are known to excel in similar areas. One of my clients, Jennifer, was the head of operations for processing insurance claims. Data showed that her department's productivity measures were less than what other companies reported. Jennifer and several of her leaders toured operations departments in similar industries and learned better ways to do things through automation and processes that supported performance measure goals. Armed with new ideas, Jennifer set innovative and realistic goals for the year. By the end of the year, her operations team had automated many manual steps using technology and had streamlined their claims processing workflow.

## SMART GOALS

You achieve the desired future state by setting goals. You've likely heard that goals should be SMART: specific, measurable, achievable, relevant, and time-bound. Specific goals are clear, leaving no room for ambiguity. The goal "Improve customer service" is unclear and vague. Rewriting this for specificity could be: "Reduce customer service complaint response to under eight business hours by March 31."

A measurable goal is one that includes criteria for tracking the outcome. In the previous example, customer service complaint response time can be measured.

An achievable goal is realistic and attainable, given the available resources. The goal "Double revenue in two months" may not be achievable. "Increase revenue by 10 percent by the end of Q1" may be more realistic.

A relevant goal is one that matters to the business or individual. It is aligned with organizational and departmental goals. "Reduce loan processing time from thirty days to twenty by year end" is relevant.

A time-bound goal includes a clear deadline for completion. This helps create a sense of urgency and progress tracking.

Additional examples of SMART goals include the following:

- Increase revenue from $100M to $130M by the end of Q4.
- Achieve a 95 percent customer success score by year end.
- Decrease the average trouble ticket resolution time from thirty minutes to twenty-five minutes by June 30.

SMART goals provide a clear understanding of what needs to be achieved by when. They serve as the foundation to know the most important work to accomplish. By tracking progress toward the goal, teams are more motivated and milestones can be celebrated.

Use SMART goals to put a stake in the ground for the desired future state you want to see at the end of a given time period to have a starting point. You can make changes, if needed, after you complete the gap analysis.

## GAP ANALYSIS

A gap analysis is used to assess the differences between the current state and the desired future state. It highlights the gaps that must be closed to reach the future state goals. Start with the current state and document the relevant information. If you have goals to increase revenue and profit, it's important to know what the current revenue and profit numbers are.

Analyze the factors that contribute to each. How many customers buy your products or services, how many are repeat customers, what is the average order size, and what products or services generate the greatest profits? From an operational performance perspective, what are production rates, cycle times, and defect rates? For skills and competencies, do you have the right people in place, or do you need more innovative thinking to reach the future state goals? Do you have the right technology solutions in place to support scalability and functionality?

Let's take the example of a product company that wants to increase sales and profitability. The gap analysis may look like this:

### Sales Metrics Gap:

- Current sales revenue: $15M versus the goal of $25M
- Current client conversion rate: 8 percent versus the goal of 12 percent
- Current average deal size: $55,000 versus the desired goal of $75,000
- Current sales cycle duration: 120 days versus the target goal of 90 days
- Current customer retention rate: 60 percent versus the goal of 80 percent

## Processes Gap:

- Current sales team CRM usage: 50 percent versus the goal of full adoption with features leveraged
- Inefficient sales processes with multiple manual steps versus streamlined, automated processes with accurate and current sales reporting

## Skills Gap:

- Limited onboarding and follow-on training for the sales team versus comprehensive training programs to support needed product knowledge
- Inability to provide consultative selling and negotiations versus experienced sales skills and product expertise

## Technology Gap:

- Current CRM implementation doesn't support sales teams' need versus a fully functional CRM with sales reporting

## Resources Gap:

- Lack of marketing support versus integrated marketing and sales efforts
- Too few salespeople versus optimal staffing levels

This example gives you a good idea of what to capture as part of your own gap analysis for your area of responsibility.

## DEFINE STRATEGIES

Once you have completed the gap analysis, it's time to determine the strategies to use to close the gap between the current state and the desired future state. For example, strategies to increase revenue could be to acquire new companies, introduce new products, expand into new global markets, hire more salespeople, or expand partnerships. Strategies to increase profitability may be to sunset old products that are expensive to maintain, bundle products and charge higher margins, sell to a new demographic that is willing to pay more, outsource functions, or streamline and automate processes to improve operational efficiencies. Strategies to improve customer satisfaction could be to shorten response times to answer client questions, provide information to help customers know how to select the right product or service, provide exceptional training on how to use the products, or personalize products.

A word of caution here. When you go through an exercise to develop a list of strategies to achieve a goal, the result may likely be a list that is much more than what can be done. Let's use the previous gap analysis example to develop a list of strategies that are possibilities for closing the gap.

## Sales Metrics Strategies:

- Implement targeted sales campaigns to increase revenue and conversion rates.
- Bundle products and services to increase deal size.
- Optimize the sales cycle with more automation and follow-up processes.

## Process Optimization Strategies:

- Automate repetitive tasks with the CRM tool.
- Provide training and mentoring on the CRM to increase its usage.

## Skills Improvement Strategies:

- Develop and implement a robust onboarding and training program to provide needed product knowledge to the sales team.
- Implement online training programs that can be viewed on-demand.

## Technology Strategy:

- Determine whether a new CRM with more functionality is needed.

## Resources Strategies;

- Recruit additional high-quality salespeople to meet staffing needs.
- Align sales team needs and marketing efforts to help drive sales.

This example highlights work that contributes to meeting the future-state revenue goals, likely more than what's possible. As a leader, you need to determine which strategies provide the highest value for meeting goals.

## PRIORITIZE THE STRATEGIES

At this point, it's time to prioritize the strategies to ensure that the most important issues are addressed first, especially when the associated work exceeds budget and resource capacity. Consider using the following factors when you're prioritizing each strategy:

- **Impact:** Will some strategies positively affect more than one area? It's a bonus when you can fix one area and solve multiple problems. For example, training programs to help salespeople be more knowledgeable may drive more sales and build trust and confidence with customers, which also increases customer satisfaction and retention. A great onboarding and training program may also make it easier to hire and retain quality salespeople.

- **Urgency:** Do some strategies need to be implemented quickly to mitigate current risks or issues?

- **Effort and resources needed:** Can some of the strategies be implemented quickly? For example, a targeted sales campaign may not require many resources and could be implemented quickly, increasing revenues.

- **Feasibility:** Is a strategy feasible given current resources and constraints? Implementing a new CRM may be a high priority, but if the sales and marketing teams are already working on other large initiatives, the resource constraints may make it unrealistic at the present time.

- **Sequence of execution:** Do one or more strategies need to be completed before another can be started? For example, if a decision is made to move to a new CRM, it may not make sense to train the sales team in the current CRM with outdated functionality.

Prioritization is an ongoing process. As you start planning the work, it's not uncommon to find that adjustments are needed along the way. What was initially a high priority may move lower on the list as you learn more about the work that is required. Or something that you deem a high priority may not be a priority at all for another department team that plays a critical role.

The important thing is to put a stake in the ground for the highest-priority goals to provide clarity, focus, and direction for both you and your team. It helps you set boundaries, deliver the highest-value work, and ensure accountability for team members. It's also foundational when you need to push back on that request to take on a new project and resources are already tapped out.

CHAPTER FOURTEEN
# PLAN THE WORK AND EXECUTE

**BRUCE, THE CEO OF A TECHNOLOGY SERVICES COMPANY,** hired me to recover a large, high-visibility program. He was recently blindsided by his program manager, Ravi, who had reported that everything had been fine until the prior month. The update at that point had been that the program was going to be late, with no estimate of how long the delay would be or what had caused it. I met with Ravi, and one of the first things he said to me was, "This program is too large to be managed using project management software. It can only be managed using spreadsheets and presentations."

From that comment, I had a pretty good understanding that little to no planning had been done. Several poor decisions were made. Executives dictated the delivery date instead of taking the time to estimate the work involved. The budget wasn't correlated with the required effort. Fifteen projects had been started at the same time, even though several were dependent on the successful completion of other projects. This caused the program to be overstaffed, and it complicated lines of communication.

I spent the next few months restructuring the program, putting several projects on hold until the prerequisite projects were completed, and working with the project managers and subject matter experts to plan out the remaining work in each area. And yes, we used project management software to develop the project schedules, interrelationships between projects, and tracking results.

Everyone was aware of the critical path of the program and each project, so we knew where to focus resources. The program was delivered on schedule and within budget. Things weren't perfect, but we had the right people and schedules to know how to optimize corrective actions.

No organization or project drifts to success. Successful leaders are intentional about achieving results and don't substitute hoping and praying for developing and executing against plans. "Failing to plan is planning to fail," said Benjamin Franklin.

Plans are the road map for providing direction and the approach toward reaching goals. They are essential for understanding resource and skill needs, establishing budgets, and prioritizing the work. Are the needed skills available, or can someone be trained? Should it be outsourced? What effect will that have on the budget and schedule? Which work has dependencies on other work? What happens if a key project is delayed? What risks must be mitigated? It's like a puzzle with lots of pieces to put in place effectively and efficiently. Without plans, the puzzle is difficult, if not impossible, to assemble.

A plan may be something as simple as listing out key milestones for work that has been done successfully in the past, following a repeatable process. This type of plan takes little effort. Other work may be more complex, like implementing a new solution across the department or multiple departments.

You may be thinking that planning is the role of a project

manager. And you're right about that. I'm not trying to turn you into a PM but to set expectations around what you need to provide your PM and what to expect from them. In the event you aren't provided a PM, you may need to fill this role, and the following information may be useful. Let's discuss types of projects and complexity.

## PROJECT FAILURE RATES

As a leader, a big part of your responsibility is to achieve results. You will likely have multiple projects to oversee to deliver value to the company. A common mistake I've seen during my career is that leaders don't understand the influence that size and complexity have on projects. Almost always, one or more of the components are underestimated for large, complex projects: the work to be performed, the number of people needed, the time it takes to complete the work, and the cost.

Research from McKinsey shows that almost half (45 percent) of large IT projects exceed the initial budget, incur schedule overruns of 7 percent, and underdeliver on the expected return on investment by 56 percent.[1]

Why is this? Multiple factors contribute to failed projects, but the most common one I see is that executives implement a one-size-fits-all approach. For example, assume your team has been assigned a project to power wash the sidewalks in a neighborhood. A team of ten people shows up with power washers and starts cleaning the sidewalks. Every section of the sidewalk that is cleaned is progress toward the end goal. If you need to finish the job faster, add more people and power washers.

This is how many people think about how to manage projects. Start working on something and add people if the schedule slips. This may work for power washing sidewalks, but it will fail miserably when dealing with projects that involve people and change.

I don't want you to think like this. Let's look at project characteristics and tactics you can implement quickly to assess the types of projects you are responsible for.

## SINGLE DEPARTMENT VERSUS CROSS-FUNCTIONAL PROJECTS

While working for a government contractor, I attended graduate classes at night to learn more about working with the federal government. Sharon, a procurement officer for one of the larger contractors, shared the following story with the class.

"I got a call from the contracting officer last week, asking me which proposal our company wanted to submit. Apparently, two different teams within the company submitted proposals without the other team knowing about it. This proposal was a huge effort. Literally hundreds of people were involved in writing the proposal over the past six months. It was also a classified project by the federal agency and had to be hand-delivered by personnel with the required security clearance. This was not a couple of boxes of documents; the proposal was delivered on three pallets. The company had to rent a truck to deliver the chaperoned pallets to the agency.

"Not only did this cause a major issue within the company, with both teams arguing over which proposal would be submitted, but also we wasted hundreds of thousands of dollars and looked incompetent in front of one of our largest clients."

I was surprised that this company didn't have better internal communications to avoid embarrassing mistakes like this. I was even more surprised to learn that it's not that uncommon.

While doing project assessments for a large insurance

company, I discovered that two separate internal teams were each developing systems to solve the same problem. More than a million dollars had been invested between the two teams, and neither was aware of the work being done by the other. When I brought this up to the CIO, he was surprised, scheduled a few meetings, and shut down one of the projects.

According to Grammarly's 2022 *State of Business Communications* report, business leaders estimate that poor communication in the workplace accounts for a loss of 7.47 hours per knowledge worker per week, costing a company more than 18 percent of the total salaries paid. That equates to $1.2 trillion lost dollars in the US alone.[2]

Self-contained projects within one department are not usually too difficult to manage and don't require a lot of formal project management practices. Examples of these types of projects include things like a marketing department implementing a content calendar for social media and email campaigns, finance conducting an internal audit to find areas for cost savings, or IT implementing a new inventory system to track hardware assets used within the company. These examples can be completed within each respective department without interfering with other areas of the company.

Cross-functional projects involve people from two or more functional areas of the organization and possibly external groups. Let's take the example of a company that wants to reduce travel expenses by standardizing vendors to negotiate better rates. This could be preferred airlines, rental car companies, and hotels where negotiated corporate rates are better than other discounted rates. This will likely affect every person in the company who travels regularly. Because it requires change, expect it to be met with resistance. Travelers have their favorite loyalty programs and want to continue accumulating miles on their favorite airline and free nights at their preferred hotel chain.

This is now a cross-functional project that involves multiple people who are affected by the change or who have a role to play in its implementation. Travelers are affected and the change needs to be dealt with. The executive team must be involved to explain why the change is needed and how it benefits the company. Another department will have to write, communicate, implement, and enforce the new travel policy. If a new travel system is required, the technology department is involved. A support desk must be equipped to answer questions when people can't book what they want and understand when exceptions are permitted.

In cross-functional projects like this, it's key for leaders to align all the affected departments and stakeholders early on to avoid sending mixed messages. When some department heads support the change and others resist it, the project is set up to fail from the start. Leaders must present a united front, reinforcing the "why" behind the decision and helping their teams shift from individual preferences to organizational priorities.

Equally important is involving key stakeholders early. Travel coordinators, frequent travelers, finance, and IT all have insight into the day-to-day impact of the change. Their feedback can help flag potential roadblocks, improve the policy, and increase adoption. When leaders recognize the cross-functional collaboration and implementation requirements of initiatives, they are much more likely to succeed, not just because of good planning but because leaders make sure people feel heard and valued along the way.

Another scenario I've seen frequently in organizations is that someone thinks a project is self-contained within their department, only to find out later that resources from other departments are needed. Say you want to use a task management software tool to track the progress of your team's work. You research available software and decide on one. Your manager approves the purchase. You want to move quickly to get it in place, so you pay for it on your credit card. This seems straightforward, since you are implementing a tool only for your department.

However, after you've made the purchase, the technology team informs you that a different software package is the company standard and that they aren't going to support multiple versions of similar tools. Procurement gets upset because they handle all software licensing, and you should've gone through them. It turns into a big headache for you and for your team.

An easy way to determine whether more than one department is involved is to complete a stakeholder matrix to ensure that you've thought through everything. I like to use a template that includes every department within a company as well as external stakeholders. Legal, compliance, security, and training departments are often the last to be included and appreciate being involved early on.

The following sample stakeholder matrix can help you determine which departments are involved in an initiative. This helps categorize stakeholders based on their level of interest and influence and how to engage with each department effectively.

| STAKEHOLDER | INTEREST LEVEL | LEVEL OF INFLUENCE |
|---|---|---|
| Executives | High | High |
| Operations | Medium | High |
| Finance | Medium | High |
| IT/Technology | High | Medium |
| Marketing | Medium | Low |
| Human Resources | Low | Medium |
| Legal/ Compliance | Low | High |
| Procurement | Medium | High |
| Sales | High | Medium |
| Customer Support | Medium | Low |
| Training | Medium | Medium |

| STAKEHOLDER | ROLE | ENGAGEMENT STRATEGY |
|---|---|---|
| Executives | Sponsor | Regular updates, involved in key decisions |
| Operations | Execution of key tasks | Frequent check-ins, involved in planning |
| Finance | Budget oversight | Monthly updates, budget approvals |
| IT/Technology | Support, infrastructure | Weekly updates, key partner for implementation |
| Marketing | Communication strategies, external messaging | Engage as needed for deliverables |
| Human Resources | Hiring, employee engagement | Keep informed, occasional feedback |
| Legal/ Compliance | Legal compliance | Inform when significant changes, seek approval as needed |
| Procurement | Vendor selection | Engage when vendors involved |
| Sales | Affected by outcomes, user of new system | Regular involvement for feedback |
| Customer Support | End user interface, new system support | Provide input from customers |
| Training | Training development for users | Engage early and keep informed of functionality |

Once you have a good idea of how many departments and individuals are involved, we need to understand the project's difficulty.

## COMPLEX VERSUS COMPLICATED PROJECTS

One of my consulting engagements was to assess a failing project that was likely heading to litigation if not turned around quickly. My client was the vendor that had agreed to provide products and services for a Fortune 50 company—services that they had not performed before and products that needed substantial changes to support the agreement.

I recall a conversation with Greg, the C-suite executive in charge of the project, who said, "I just don't understand. This is the first project that we haven't been able to grind our way through. Sure, we've been late on projects before, but we've been able to figure it out eventually."

You don't grind your way through complex projects. This is a formula for a lawsuit if you're dealing with an external client.

As mentioned earlier, many managers tend to believe that larger cross-functional projects can be handled the same way as a departmental project. Just work harder and put a few more people on the project.

Let's take a minute to discuss the difference between *complicated* and *complex*, as these two words are frequently used interchangeably. Complicated means that something has many difficult parts to understand, but these parts can be figured out. Complicated work can be planned out by methodically breaking down its components until each one is understood. Complex, on the other hand, is when things are not only difficult but also have higher interrelatedness and intricacies. It refers to a situation where a project or situation is intertwined in such a way that makes it harder to understand with multiple options.

For example, assume your team is responsible for updating and standardizing the computer software in your company of one thousand employees. This is a complicated project, but with effort, it can be broken down into its component parts and planned out. Once the process has been refined, it's no more difficult to update two thousand computers than one thousand. It may just take longer or require additional resources.

Deciding to replace the financial system across an organization is complex, involving multifaceted organizational needs. It encompasses multiple software integrations internally and externally; changes to intricate business processes and procedures across multiple departments; stakeholder alignment both inside and outside the company; organizational change management; potential changes to needed skills; data migration from existing systems; compliance, regulatory, and cybersecurity needs; testing and piloting before a complete rollout; communications to keep everyone informed; user training and help desk support; and scope management.

You'll want to understand the difference between complicated and complex work and plan for it accordingly. When responsible for a complex initiative, staff it with program or project managers who have done this type of work before. *Grinding your way through* is not a good approach.

## POSITIONING PROJECTS FOR SUCCESS FROM THE START

I've completed hundreds of project reviews and assessments and can tell if they have a good chance of being successfully completed based on how the project was set up in the beginning. I've also spent a lot of time recovering projects that had gone off the rails. Project failures can be mitigated by taking the time up front to make the right decisions. The more complex the project or initiative, the more important it is to put the right people, tools, and controls in place in the beginning.

The following checklist will help you set your project up to be successful:

| YES | NO | DESCRIPTION |
|:---:|:---:|---|
| ☐ | ☐ | Do I have a good understanding of the business case and objectives for the project and why it's important? |
| ☐ | ☐ | Do I know who has decision-making authority (who can approve budgets, changes, resources)? |
| ☐ | ☐ | Is the project aligned with the appropriate organizational and departmental goals? |
| ☐ | ☐ | Do I have a good understanding of the scope and complexity of the project? |
| ☐ | ☐ | Is the right executive sponsor assigned to the project? |

| YES | NO | DESCRIPTION |
|:---:|:---:|---|
| ☐ | ☐ | Does the executive sponsor understand their roles and responsibilities? |
| ☐ | ☐ | Does the executive sponsor have the needed time to dedicate to the project? |
| ☐ | ☐ | Do I have measures in place to track progress against objectives? |
| ☐ | ☐ | Do I know who all the key stakeholders are for the project and their interests? |
| ☐ | ☐ | Do I have a communications plan for all stakeholders? |
| ☐ | ☐ | Is a project manager with the right experience assigned to manage the project? |
| ☐ | ☐ | Are all the needed resources (people, tools, budget) available for the project? |
| ☐ | ☐ | Do all the team members understand their roles and responsibilities? |
| ☐ | ☐ | Is this project's priority clearly communicated to the leadership team and to all stakeholders? |

| YES | NO | DESCRIPTION |
|:---:|:---:|:---|
| ☐ | ☐ | Has a project kickoff meeting been held (or scheduled) to set resources, budget, and schedule expectations and to align stakeholders? |
| ☐ | ☐ | Is the project schedule realistic, based on scope and requirements? |
| ☐ | ☐ | Do I have a risk management plan in place to identify, communicate, and mitigate risks? |
| ☐ | ☐ | Do I have access to needed subject matter experts when necessary? |
| ☐ | ☐ | Do project team members understand the reporting structure of the project? |
| ☐ | ☐ | Do I have a realistic project budget, including a buffer for unexpected costs? |
| ☐ | ☐ | Is an escalation process in place to address situations outside my control? |
| ☐ | ☐ | Do I have the right project metrics in place to track schedule progress? |

## EXECUTE AND TRACK PROGRESS

Plans serve as the foundation for needed resources, a baseline for the scope of work to be performed, and the schedule for completion to deliver a return on investment. As work is completed, be sure to celebrate key milestones with the team. Recognize the contributions of team members to keep employee engagement and morale high and momentum going. This is covered in more detail in chapter 9.

A best practice is to hold weekly project status meetings to understand what work was planned versus completed, share updates on risks and issues, and review staffing needs. You'll also see schedule and budget trends that may trigger the need for corrective action. As the leader, meet with your PM to ensure that you are provided the needed information to know whether the project is tracking to be a success. Keep in mind that a successful project is one that delivers the expected return on investment, not just one that is on schedule and within budget. If the scope of work is reduced to meet a deadline, the return on investment may also be reduced.

Most all projects of any size or complexity encounter problems. The key is to anticipate issues as early as possible when it's likely easier to address them. Don't wait until the project is adversely affected. Explain to your PM the need to communicate concerns quickly. And remember, don't shoot the messenger when you're given news you don't want to hear.

Don't leave project execution to chance. Work with your PM to understand challenges, the obstacles you may need to remove, where constraints exist, and dependencies on other projects. Otherwise, you may get blindsided and, even worse, blindside your manager and executives with bad news. No executive likes surprises such as missing a date and not knowing about it until the last minute.[3]

Planning and executing are hard. Few companies excel in prioritizing their projects and delivering the return on investment on schedule and within budget. You will be ahead of most people by understanding the type of project you are dealing with and following the checklist for setting up your projects for success from the start.

Goal setting and execution both require much thought, planning, and collaboration. You will continue to improve these skills over time. No one gets everything right the first, second, or third time. Even after you think you have priorities set and work planned out, things will likely change. You'll need to course-correct. The key is following proven processes and frameworks so that you can be proactive and make intentional changes instead of being reactive.

Awareness

Effective
Communication

**Lead by
Example**

High-
Performing
Teams

Exceptional
Results

Productivity
Habits

# PART SIX

---

# HIGH-PERFORMING TEAMS

People are not your most important asset.
The right people are.

**—JIM COLLINS**

**THE FOUNDATION OF ANY SUCCESSFUL** organization is its people. High-performing teams don't happen by chance—they are intentionally built through thoughtful hiring, development, and leadership practices. As a leader, your ability to attract, retain, and develop the right talent directly influences your team's performance and ultimately contributes to the overall success of the organization.

Far too often, hiring managers don't hire the best people because they are focused on filling positions quickly rather than strategically. Tight timelines, pressure from senior leaders, and overwhelming workloads cause them to prioritize availability over ability. Also, my experience is that many hiring managers lack a clear, structured process for identifying top talent and rely instead on surface-level impressions or gut feelings during interviews. Over time, a culture of mediocrity emerges, and average performance becomes the norm.

It's hard work to build and retain a team of A-players, but it's worth the effort. As a leader, your ability to deliver exceptional results through others depends on the quality of your team. Let's look at how to put a team of high performers in place.

# CHAPTER FIFTEEN

# COMPANIES BECOME WHO THEY HIRE

**A COMPANY IS ONLY AS STRONG** as the people it hires. Every hire shapes the culture, productivity, and future of the organization. Hiring top talent isn't just a nice-to-have; it's a strategic imperative. We learned in chapter 2 that people mimic the leader. If you hire leaders who are mediocre performers, expect them to hire the same caliber of person.

Mediocre hires cost more than you realize. They drain time, resources, and energy, dragging down the performance and morale of the entire team or department. They make excuses for why they can't complete their work and blame others for their shortcomings.

Wouldn't you rather hire top talent who elevate your team, drive innovation and productivity, and help others excel? That makes your job so much easier.

## CHARACTERISTICS OF HIGH-PERFORMING TEAMS

High-performing teams have distinct characteristics that set them apart from teams with a mediocre culture.

The first is trust and respect—for you (as the leader) and one another. People get along, pitch in and help each other out when needed, and work toward achieving common goals. No one spends time second-guessing why someone did something. Trust also promotes better communications across the team, making it easier to share ideas and feedback without worrying about being judged. Trust and respect create a culture with less stress and anxiety while building psychological safety.

Accountability is expected on high-performing teams. Everyone does their fair share and takes responsibility for their actions and outcomes. Rather than make excuses or place blame, they work together to find solutions.

High performers also require clarity on goals and expectations and the autonomy to get the work done. They don't need or want to be micromanaged. And they want constructive feedback to use for improvement and growth and to build a culture of excellence.

Remember, people mimic the leader, so it's important that you set the example of the characteristics of an A-player.

## ONE B-PLAYER CAN WRECK THE CULTURE

I was once on the interview panel for a director-level role on a sales team at a client company. We interviewed several qualified applicants during the week and provided detailed feedback that the recruiter could use to narrow the final list to two to three candidates.

I was surprised that the VP of sales, Darren, seemed to like candidates who others on the interview team felt were weaker. I called him to get more information on his reasoning. "I have a question on the interview feedback you provided. It seems like you're leaning toward candidates who aren't as strong as the others. What am I missing?"

Darren said, "I think the candidates who you and the others like are overqualified. Most of them do what I do." I continued to ask questions about the top two candidates the others on the interview panel liked. I finally got to the real issue. "I hired a really good person one time," he said. "She was so good, in fact, that she replaced me, and I was fired from the company. I'll never do that again."

Do you hire people who are more skilled and smarter than you? You may feel intimidated or threatened by someone who is more capable or knowledgeable than you, like Darren did. This feeling is understandable when you think about how our brains work, looking for threats to our well-being. This is another one of those times when our two-hundred-thousand-year-old DNA doesn't serve us.

Great leaders hire the best people because they know that if their team is successful, they will be too. Morale, employee engagement, and productivity go up, and turnover goes down. Your culture is based on who you have on the team and the examples you set as a leader.

Nick Saban, former head football coach at the University of Alabama, says, "Mediocre people don't like high achievers, and high achievers don't like mediocre people." He continues by describing his team goals for spring practice. "Get the right guys on the bus, get them in the right seats, and get the wrong guys off the bus. You can never have any team chemistry in your organization until everyone is committed to the same standards and the same things."

Let's define A-players, B-players, and C-players. A-players, referred to by Saban as high achievers, are ambitious and in it for the long haul. They are intentional in their commitment to being their highest-performing self. They establish routines and habits to optimize their efficiency and their health. Contrary to what some people think, these people are not workaholics. They focus on how to bring their best selves to the job at hand. They understand the importance of taking care of themselves. These people are avid learners who want to master their skills. They have a growth mindset and want to develop their potential. They are willing to do what it takes to develop their craft.

A-players tend to fall into two categories: (1) the person who wants to be the best at their craft and (2) the person who wants to be on the rocket trajectory with their career and aspires to keep growing in many new areas.

For example, someone's superpower may be to underwrite mortgage loans, paint beautiful pictures, or recruit top talent, but they aren't interested in managing an underwriting department, owning an art gallery, or becoming the head of HR. They love what they do and excel at it. Others may be more interested in climbing the corporate ladder and moving up in the organization.

B-players meet the requirements of their job but seldom go above and beyond. They don't take the initiative to help others or solve problems. They may learn new things by attending training but seldom put that knowledge into practice. They do their job—nothing more, nothing less. For the most part, they do mediocre work and propagate a culture of mediocrity.

C-players do the bare minimum to keep from getting fired. They do their best to fly under the radar so that they aren't called out. They don't invest in themselves to learn new things. C-players are disengaged. They don't like being held accountable and make excuses for low performance. They may not play nicely with others and have a negative attitude that drags others down.

Why am I defining these terms? Because it's important to understand that it's impossible to build high-performing teams when you have B- or C-players in key roles.

A-players hire only more A-players, while B-players hire more B-players and C-players, and a culture of mediocrity follows. One B-player drags the entire team down. How is it that a person like this can have such a negative impact?

In the book *School Culture Rewired*, authors Steve Gruenert and Todd Whitaker write, "The culture of any organization is shaped by the worst behavior the leader is willing to tolerate."[1] Let that sink in for a minute. Leaders aren't defined by their values but by the behaviors they tolerate. If you tolerate B- or C-players, you've just lowered the bar for your team. Your A-players will be frustrated and likely start looking for another job. Team morale heads south. As the leader, your credibility is called into question and the downward spiral starts.

The first tactic to use for high-performing teams is to hire the best people, even when they are smarter than you. This may feel a bit unnerving at first, but the rewards will far outweigh the discomfort.

## A-PLAYERS ARE FREE

You may be thinking that having a team of A-players would be awesome. Who wouldn't want to lead a team that gets along well, solves problems, and achieves results without a lot of oversight? You may also be thinking that a team of high achievers must cost a lot and wouldn't fit into your budget. Let's think about this differently.

A coaching client, Travis, was the leader of a technology team responsible for the global implementation of a large software system. During one of our calls, he said, "I have a limited budget and can only hire contractors who don't have the level of expertise I need."

"How many people are on the team, and what is your budget?" I asked.

"Four people and $85 per hour." If you do the math for a year based on 2,000 hours, that comes out to $680,000.

"What rate do you need to pay to get the skills you need?" He replied, "Around $125 per hour."

"What if you replaced your four $85 per hour contractors with two $125 per hour contractors? That would be $500,000 per year, and you'd get more work and save $180,000."

Travis was skeptical at first but, after thinking about it, said he would try it. A couple of months later, we had a much different call. "The two rock stars I hired are doing way more work than all four of the ones I had. I can offload more complex work to them, and they get it done right and quickly. I have more time now to work on strategy and the business."

According to McKinsey's 2023 State of Organizations report, the high performers of high-complexity work are 800 percent more productive than average workers in the same role.[2] That is a huge delta! Let's say you have a rock star financial analyst who is five times more productive than an average financial analyst. You don't pay the rock star five times more than the average analyst. I've yet to see salary bands in companies that have a range of 800 percent. That would be like saying the annual salary range for an engineer is between $100,000 and $800,000.

Sabrina Starling, PhD, author of *How to Hire the Best: The*

*Entrepreneur's Ultimate Guide to Attracting Top Performing Team Members*, writes that she has seen that one A-player can do the work of nine to twelve average people.[3]

And it's not just about the money. A-players attract other A-players, making it easier to hire top talent into your company. A-players solve their own problems instead of bringing them to you to solve. They make fewer mistakes, reducing rework. They drive innovation. They hold themselves and others accountable. They set a positive example for the rest of the team.

Now you know that A-players cost less than B-players, get more done, and uplift the team. This makes everyone look good. Hiring smart people, even when they are smarter than you, is the right tactic for building your high-performing team. According to various leaders, "If you're the smartest person in the room, you're in the wrong room."

## INTERVIEWING AND SELECTION

Darren Hardy, former publisher of *Success Magazine*, tells the story of interviewing former Ritz-Carlton cofounder and president Horst Schulze. "How do you train your employees to be so friendly?" Hardy asked.

Schulze replied, "We don't hire people in the hotel business and teach them how to be friendly. We hire friendly people and teach them the hotel business."

Most people focus primarily on hiring for the needed skills without considering the characteristics important to a specific role. For example, characteristics of A-players include respect for others, high personal and professional standards, self-motivation, a growth mindset, helping others, and lifelong learning, to name a few. A customer service role requires someone who is friendly, patient, and likes helping others. A project manager must be detail oriented, motivating, reasonable, willing to push back, able to have difficult conversations, and positive. You miss a critical first step if you leave out the needed characteristics in a job description that contribute to success.

If you value information sharing across the team, you can ask candidates to provide examples of how they shared what they learned with team members in previous roles. Or perhaps you expect team members to be proactive and solve problems. Ask for examples where the candidate has taken the initiative when they've encountered issues. This also helps set the stage for how a candidate needs to perform in their role to be successful.

Now that you've taken care of the necessary characteristics, be clear about the needed skills, experience, and requirements. For example, instead of saying you require experience with spreadsheets, elaborate on that. Do you need someone who can do pivot tables and data analysis, or someone who can use it for tracking? Work with your HR partner/recruiter to provide the required information and to understand how the recruiting process works at your organization.

I've consulted in several companies where it seemed like the interviewers were just winging it, making up interview questions on the fly. Hiring the right people for your team is a critical leadership role. Be intentional about planning for the best candidate interview experience that provides you with the necessary information to determine whether they should be selected.

Partner with a good recruiter who will identify the best approach for conducting candidate interviews. This person will help you establish an interview panel and assign topic areas and questions for each person to cover. For example, one person interviews specifically for things like characteristics, emotional intelligence, and culture fit; another covers topics related to the requisite job skills; and someone else asks questions related to handling different types of situations. Each interviewer should know the questions they want to ask for their topic area(s) in advance so that the same questions aren't asked multiple times, like "So why are you looking?"

Interviewers should document the results of the interviews and provide specific feedback to the recruiter and hiring manager. The feedback needs to be more than "I really liked Jacqueline" or "Don was a great communicator."

An example of feedback for a candidate who was a good communicator includes comments like this: "Don communicated his ideas concisely and clearly. He gave thoughtful examples that were easily understandable. He held eye contact when asked a question and spoke confidently in his responses. He listened carefully when asked a question and asked for clarification if he didn't understand it fully. He answered the questions that were asked, without going off on tangents. The conversation was engaging, and he had a sense of humor. Don came to the interview prepared and had a list of questions he wanted to ask."

See the difference?

# CHAPTER SIXTEEN
# EMPLOYEE RETENTION

**KATE HAS ALWAYS BEEN AN A-PLAYER.** As a data analyst for the same company for six years, she had worked in every product group, provided insights into analytics that generated hundreds of millions of dollars in revenue, won several awards, was promoted many times, and led a small team.

Then her career started to stagnate. Her manager, Ellen, had told her a year ago that she was next in line for her job and was just waiting for her manager, Keith, to retire. What Ellen didn't realize was that boredom was a nonstarter for A-players. Kate had taken on several outside leadership roles as a board member and helped organize high-profile events for executive women.

It was only a matter of time until Kate's value was seen by others in her industry. She was approached by a top-tier company looking for a vice president to lead an underperforming department, two career levels from where she had been for the last two years. After interviewing with the executive team, Kate realized that the new company had much greater advancement opportunities; invested heavily in the growth and development of its leaders; and had a more forward-thinking, mature leadership team.

Kate had always been a loyal employee and appreciated the training and recognition she had received thus far. However, she knew that the new company would offer better career and growth opportunities. She would be surrounded by more innovative people who could keep her challenged.

When she resigned, Ellen and Keith were shocked. They offered her more money to stay and another team to manage. It was too little, too late. It shouldn't take a resignation to get the attention of company leaders to take care of their employees, especially the high achievers.

Who do you have on your team who is or could be an A-player? Are you doing everything you can to keep them motivated and engaged?

As you have already learned, the ability to keep employees engaged and motivated comes down to you. It's up to you to provide a safe and positive work environment to retain employees. This starts with the first impression made during an interview and continues through the onboarding process.

## ONBOARDING

"I don't have a laptop," Teri said to Bryan, the hiring manager, on her first day on the job. Bryan embarked on a search to contact the technology team responsible for remote employee equipment delivery. After several hours, he learned that the equipment had not been sent out, and he submitted an expedited delivery request. Three days later, Teri received her computer, monitor, and login information.

According to a Gallup poll, only 12 percent of new hires surveyed reported a good onboarding process at their organization.[4] The Society for Human Resource Management reports that 69 percent of employees who had exceptional onboarding experiences are likely to have at least a three-year tenure with their company and experience 50 percent greater new-hire productivity.[5] According to *Harvard Business Review*, one out of five new hires leaves within forty-five days of a new job. A negative onboarding experience contributes to this high turnover.[6]

Retaining high-performing team members is critical for your leadership success. Several factors contribute to this, starting with onboarding the new hire's first impression of the company, and play a critical role in whether they will be successful.

A new hire may feel particularly vulnerable after accepting an offer with your company. Will I fit in with the team? How will I be perceived by other team members? Will I be able to ramp up quickly? What will be expected of me the first week? The first month? How well do people collaborate? Who will help me get up to speed? How much training will I get/need to be able to do my job? How will my performance be evaluated? What is the dress code? Will I get a list of who to contact when I have questions?

In your leadership role, strive to answer these types of questions in advance to help reduce the anxiety and stress that accompany starting a new job. Provide a great onboarding experience. How a new person is indoctrinated will factor into their company loyalty and tenure.

Here are a few tips to consider.

- **Congratulate the new hire.** Reach out to the new hire after the offer has been accepted to welcome them to the team. It's surprising how this small gesture can put someone's mind at ease and start building the feeling of belonging. You may want to have other team members do the same. Once the new hire accepts your offer, they may get a counteroffer when they resign from their current company. You want them to feel a part of your team so that the counter isn't as attractive.

- **Send company stuff.** Send the new hire a swag bag of goodies, welcoming them to the team. Include things with company logos to help them start feeling like part of the team (T-shirts, coffee mugs, water bottles, notepads). You may also want to include a book or two that the team has read or that you find helpful. Simple, inexpensive gifts go a long way toward providing a great onboarding experience. Maybe you don't have a budget for swag. That happens. Keep in mind the expense and time it takes to hire an employee. Maybe it's just a card signed by you and your team welcoming them to the group.

- **Send equipment on time.** If the role requires equipment, such as a laptop and monitor, make sure it arrives on time with the proper software installed and with clear instructions on how to set it up. Include a number to call if assistance is needed. Prior to the start date, ensure that the equipment has arrived and see if there are any additional questions.

- **Remove barriers.** Help the new hire be successful by providing the needed training and introduce them to coworkers and others to start building relationships. Some companies assign an onboarding buddy to help navigate things like who to call for what, where to find things on the intranet and other places, and to answer questions that may arise. As a leader, it's incumbent on you to ensure that the sourcing, hiring, and onboarding processes are in place to support building the best team possible.

Invest the time in your new hires to make them feel welcome. This applies to people who may be new to your team but not to the company. Welcome them to the team and help them be successful.

## EARLY WINS FOR NEW HIRE SUCCESS

Have you ever wondered why, at the beginning of the season, college sports teams play those they can easily beat? The reason is based on the winner effect, a phenomenon in which winning in one area boosts confidence and performance in other areas, creating a positive feedback loop. In a nutshell, the more you win, the more you are likely to win again.

When a person completes a job successfully, it's viewed as a win, and the brain releases dopamine, the feel-good hormone. Repeated early wins cause the continued release of dopamine, and the brain structure changes over time. A person starts to develop the mindset of being a winner.

Just like with sports teams, you can use the winner effect to position your new hire as a winner. Assign a job or task that they can accomplish within a few days. Examples you may consider for early wins include things like this:

- Provide feedback and suggestions for improvement on their onboarding experience.

- Develop a report using a dataset and provide an analysis of the results.
- Document or update a process that could be improved or streamlined.
- Assign them to handle straightforward customer service requests.

As your new employees successfully complete assignments, provide recognition for their achievements. When you set your team members up for success, you're also building their self-confidence, morale, and motivation.

What could you assign to a person who is new to the company to leverage the winner effect? These simple tactics are easy to implement and make a big difference. Remember, leadership is tactical.

## EMPLOYEE ENGAGEMENT

Gartner, a leading consulting firm, defines employee engagement as employees feeling energized, finding purpose in their work, and feeling empowered to do valuable work. A Gartner survey from June 2023 of approximately thirty-five hundred employees found that those who are excited about their work are 31 percent more likely to stay at their company, 31 percent more likely to go above and beyond what is expected, and contribute 15 percent more. Now for the bad news. Gartner research finds that only 31 percent of employees are engaged, enthusiastic, and energized in their work.[7]

Gallup's State of the Global Workplace: 2024 report shows that 33 percent of the employees in the United States and Canada were engaged in 2023, which is an increase of 2 percent from the previous year. This means that two-thirds of employees are disengaged (doing the bare minimum to keep from getting fired—the C-players) or actively disengaged (bad-mouthing the company and acting out their unhappiness). Gallup research also reports that 38 percent of employees are engaged after six months on the job and only 22 percent are engaged after three years.[8]

These statistics are not stacked in your favor. As a leader, you want to build a culture where employees are engaged and feel like they are a part of the team. We know that engaged employees are more productive, experience less burnout, and stay longer in organizations. You've already started building the right environment by hiring the best candidates, even when they are smarter than you, and providing a great onboarding experience. The challenge is keeping employees engaged for the long haul, after the onboarding honeymoon has ended.

What can you do to keep your team members engaged, especially in remote and hybrid environments? Much of this has been covered in earlier chapters, and now we can put all the tactics together.

First and foremost, build a psychologically safe work environment and create a sense of belonging.

Align work with what employees like to do. You may have someone on your team who hates dealing with spreadsheets and someone else who loves them. Some people don't like to write documentation, but others love it. Structure work so that each person is assigned tasks that are most meaningful to them. This doesn't mean that everyone gets to work on only those things they like. That's not realistic, as we all must do things we don't like. But you can find opportunities to optimize work assignments based on what team members enjoy the most if you are intentional about it.

Build authentic relationships with your employees and check in regularly. The one-on-one meeting is a great way to stay connected, show that you care, elicit feedback, and build trust.

Show appreciation to your team members. Everyone likes to be appreciated for their efforts.

Set clear expectations so that employees know how they are performing toward goals. Clarity makes it much easier to know when something is completed. See chapter 13 for more information on setting expectations.

Keep your team in the know by cascading organizational messages, providing updates on progress toward goals, and keeping them informed of upcoming initiatives. This is covered in more detail in chapter 8.

Ensure that employees have the tools they need to do their work. If working remotely, provide the necessary technology equipment, such as dual monitors, a headset, a printer, a laptop, and such. Some companies offer financial assistance for standing desks and ergonomic chairs.

Host different social events for team members to see the personal sides of their colleagues.

Encourage work-life balance. In today's world, where many employees are working from home, the work-life balance becomes a blur. Set boundaries around work and family time and model this behavior yourself.

One of the most important factors in building a culture of engagement is developing your employees and providing growth opportunities. Let's take a deeper look at this.

## EMPLOYEE DEVELOPMENT AND GROWTH

Some bosses take the position that it's the employee's responsibility to develop themselves. I don't disagree that we all need to be accountable for our continued learning, but leaders can help shape and accelerate a development path.

You may be thinking, *I don't have a training budget* or *Our training department doesn't provide the kind of training my team needs* or *We don't have time for training.* Growth opportunities don't have to cost much money. Like our health, either take the time to get healthy now or pay ten times as much (or more) later. As Mahatma Gandhi said, "Those who think they have no time for healthy eating will sooner or later have to find time for illness." Or in the context of this section: Those who think they don't have time to provide growth opportunities for their teams will have to find time later for recruiting and onboarding the replacement of someone who left for another company that did.

Growth opportunities for team members are part of your leadership role. Coaching is a great way to help team members set and reach their goals. Using one-on-one meetings is a perfect opportunity to understand employees' career aspirations, help them put a career development plan in place, and guide them on their journey. A caring leader who is willing to help goes a long way toward employee engagement and loyalty.

Group coaching is another way to encourage team growth. For example, when a problem surfaces, you can convene the team to define the problem statement, develop solutions, and facilitate reaching the best decision. Often the leader feels that it's their responsibility to solve the problem instead of using the situation as a learning opportunity for the team.

Lessons learned meetings, also called retrospectives, during and after a project are a helpful way to provide improvements across one or more teams. These meetings focus on refining the way work is done in the future without finger-pointing or placing blame. They are a safe space to offer better ways of doing things.

One of my personal favorites is to lead a book study for the team. For example, if a team needs to improve communications, an hour-long book study each week is a nonthreatening way to provide ideas and ways to improve. Each person has an opportunity to discuss the key takeaways from the book reading assignment and to suggest how to implement the ideas. This generates a lot of great discussion and allows everyone to interact in ways to continue building relationships.

Maybe you're wondering, *How do I lead a book study? What books should I consider? Are some books better than others?* Don't overcomplicate it. Select a good book for discussions, have everyone get a copy, put a schedule together with the chapter due dates, and then schedule the meetings. Let everyone know that they're expected to bring one key takeaway from the chapter for each meeting. You'll be surprised by the ideas participants share and how the team works together to implement them.

After you've led one or two book studies, ask if there are others on the team who might like to lead one to provide a growth opportunity for them.

Lunch and learns are also helpful to team members and provide an opportunity to practice presentation skills while imparting knowledge to others who are interested in the topic.

If there is a budget for attending conferences and training, be sure that attendees maximize the investment. For example, if only one or two people are sent to a conference or training class, ask them to present what they learned to a larger group when they get back. This encourages being intentional about what the attendee learns and helps focus on areas that could benefit more people.

As a leader, you may be in a unique position to see opportunities within your department or in other groups that would benefit a team member. Consider experiences you can provide to your employees to help them continue to grow in their personal career goals.

Help your team members network. Introduce them to others in the company and highlight their skills. If your department provides a useful service to others, ask another department leader if it would be helpful to have someone from your team take a few minutes during one of their meetings to provide an overview of what they do and how to improve the service.

The time and money invested in personal growth and development pay huge dividends. If you select only one or two of these tactics, your team will have meaningful growth opportunities.

## HIRE SLOW, FIRE FAST

Despite going through a rigorous hiring process and making the best decision we can on the candidate selection, we still hire people who aren't a good fit for the team or organization. Bad hires are a fact of business life, and we've all been there. Maybe someone is talented and gets things done but creates a toxic environment for teammates. Or the person turns out not to be a good culture fit, regardless of all the effort expended during the interviewing process.

A common scenario I see in companies is the belief that if a person gets results, has a specialized skill, or has deep company knowledge but has toxic behavior, they should be tolerated. Maybe that worked when a command-and-control leadership style was prevalent, but it doesn't work today. Everyone deserves to be treated respectfully. A person can't be an A-player if they are disrespectful and berate or bully others.

In other situations, a person isn't as aligned with the company or team values and culture as they portrayed in an interview. I've hired several project managers who seemed to be the right person to lead projects, but they didn't work out. Some were overly demanding when it came to deadlines and didn't take the time to understand the issues or the work involved. "The business case is due next Friday. Do whatever you need to do to make that happen. Just get it done." What level of quality do you think the business case would have? It may not be accurate or useful. Another project manager unilaterally decided he didn't need to use project management software because he could manage the tasks and resources in his head. During the interview he said he was an expert in project management software but failed to mention that he didn't use it.

Perhaps you have someone on your team who doesn't seem to be engaged and makes excuses for why they are repeatedly late delivering their work products. Or maybe someone oversold their skills and can't do the job after all.

As soon as you know the person isn't going to work out, it's time to follow a termination process. Different companies require different steps to fire someone. Partner with your HR department to follow the right process.

If the advice to hire slow and fire fast seems a little harsh to you, let's put it in context. The fallout from dragging out the inevitable creates a lot of damage. First, everyone is aware of the issue and watching to see how you will address it. If you don't resolve it properly, you lose credibility and trust as a leader. The team culture you've worked hard to build starts to crack. Second, why would you keep someone in a role and cause the rest of the team to be frustrated or slowed down in their efforts? It's not fair to the team members who want to get things done but are hindered because of a bad hire. Lastly, you aren't doing the struggling employee any favors by keeping them in the wrong role and continuing to provide negative feedback. That doesn't show compassion for the person. They deserve to be in a position where they can succeed. As Darren Hardy, author and business success coach, says, "Liberate them back to the marketplace."

If you're hoping that a person will miraculously turn around, remember this quote from Maya Angelou: "When someone shows you who they are, believe them the first time." Believe them the *first* time.

Firing someone should be done considerately and humanely. Part ways so that the employee can move on with their career and you can find the right replacement. Work with your HR department to follow the proper termination process.

No one likes to fire a person. It's not easy to have a difficult conversation to let someone go. At the end of the day, however, it's your role as the leader to do the right thing for the company and for your teams. Doing the right thing doesn't make it easy.

## PEOPLE QUIT MANAGERS, NOT COMPANIES

I interviewed a lot of people while writing this book, and it seems that just about everyone had a story about a bad boss. Caitlin, a mid-level manager, described her situation like this: "I worked for a director, Eric, who was great. He cared about the people on his team. He made sure we all worked on things that aligned with our skills and career goals. We had a training budget to ensure we got the instruction we needed to continue growing. We were all given the autonomy to do our job, including a chance to fail. He led by example and modeled the behavior he wanted to see in his team members. Then I was moved to a different part of the company, reporting to a VP of compliance. This manager, Richard, was the complete opposite. He almost always canceled our one-on-one meetings and seemed to avoid getting to know his team members. He would throw me under the bus when he was asked questions by his superiors that he couldn't answer, saying that I didn't provide updates. Each week, I gave Richard a detailed status on all the projects I was working on, highlighting key dates and where I needed help. He would call me at all hours of the night, expecting me to answer his questions at midnight or over weekends.

"He always needed to be the smartest person in the room and was quick to chastise people in meetings if he didn't like their answer. I went from feeling confident in my abilities to having no self-esteem while working for him. After three years, the negative environment was affecting my health, and I decided it was time to leave the company. Others on the team had left before I did, also fed up with Richard. No one should have to experience the condescending behavior that makes you lose confidence."

You likely have your own version of Caitlin's story. I certainly have my share of them. These are glaring behavioral issues that cause people to leave the company or find another area of the organization to work in.

Leadership development is a lifelong journey. For me, I had to learn that getting results took me only so far. I had to understand the importance of the people aspect if I wanted to progress in my career. Every chapter in this book includes the tactics that I've learned through experience, trial and error, observation, training, and reading, curating the most useful ones. My intent with this book is to help accelerate your leadership development by providing the practical resources you need to be a trusted leader who delivers results and makes a difference in the lives of others.

CONCLUSION

# CHANGING LIVES

**I HAD JUST STARTED A NEW CLIENT ENGAGEMENT,** and after a couple of days in, I noticed something unusual—most of the employees left the office early one afternoon. Curious, I asked where everyone had gone. A colleague explained that they left to be there for Chuck, a long-tenured sales employee who had come home from the hospital to live out his final days. It was clear to me that he was no ordinary employee.

When I learned more about Chuck, I was struck by the depth of his influence. His name came up in conversations, not because of the sales numbers—although those were impressive—but because of the way he made people feel. Chuck wasn't a formal leader with people reporting to him, yet he exemplified everything great leadership is about.

Olivia, a senior executive at the company, told me, "When I moved here for the job, I didn't know anyone. Chuck invited me, my husband, and my three-year-old daughter to his neighborhood for Halloween and to attend a cul-de-sac party. I remember thinking, *How generous, kind, and loving of him to invite a total stranger and my family to his house, open his doors and neighborhood, and let my daughter go trick-or-treating with his family and friends.* It was such a kind and thoughtful gesture, but what made it even more special was that, unbeknownst to us, my husband and I had just signed a contract to build a house on his street a week earlier. That invitation was the beginning of knowing Chuck not just as a coworker but also as a neighbor."

Chuck's kindness extended to his friends, neighbors, and coworkers. He hosted annual Friendsgiving gatherings at Thanksgiving, invited colleagues to go with him on sales calls to help them learn how to improve, and looked for ways to uplift others. "He wasn't just focused on his success," Olivia said. "He wanted everyone around him to succeed as well."

Owen, Chuck's former manager, shared how much he learned from him. "Chuck was my first hire, and I was terrible at leading back then. One day, Chuck pulled me aside and said, 'I appreciate the job and working here, but my job is to make you look good. I need you to know that. You're my boss, and I don't want your job. I respect you and am focused on making you look good.' This was Chuck's way of telling me to get off his back. The truth of the matter was that I micromanaged him. After that conversation, I noticed that he recognized challenges I didn't even see and was quite capable of doing his job. It took me several years to realize that Chuck had told me I was doing a bad job as a leader without telling me I was doing a bad job. He looked for ways to help people improve in a constructive way."

Chuck excelled in sales, consistently ranking as one of the company's top performers. But his real gift was his ability to connect with people. "He had no concept of time when he was talking with someone," Owen said. "If you were with Chuck, you were the most important person in the world. He gave you his full attention, not matter what else was going on."

At the heart of Chuck's life was his wife and children. When he was home, he was a dad and a husband, first and foremost, present for his family. He balanced family time with his busy travel and work schedule, never forgetting that they came first.

Chuck continued his successful track record with the company until he was diagnosed with leukemia. When one of the treatment options was a bone marrow transplant, more than three hundred people volunteered to be tested to determine whether they were a match for him. A donor was identified, and Chuck had the bone marrow transplant procedure. It was successful for a while, but the leukemia came back soon after, more aggressively than before.

Still, Chuck stayed positive and upbeat. Despite the grueling treatments, he remained a source of encouragement for everyone around him. He continued to walk his dog to the neighborhood mailboxes, always smiling, even though his body was noticeably changing as the cancer continued to spread. He remained an inspiration to coworkers, sending them uplifting notes or stopping by the office, when his health permitted, to cheer everyone on. When he had to wear an eye patch due to radiation damage, he would joke about it to put the other person at ease.

When the inevitable end was near, Chuck was released from the hospital and sent home to spend his remaining time in hospice care. The company employees wanted to honor him. They didn't want to overwhelm him or make it about them; they just wanted to show him that they cared about and loved him.

On the day Chuck was transported from the hospital to his house via ambulance, his colleagues coordinated with his wife to be there upon his arrival. Employees lined the street on both sides with signs relaying their love and admiration for him, clapping for him as the ambulance drove up.

As the medics carefully carried Chuck inside and placed him in his bed, he knew his coworkers were there to say their goodbyes and to share a final moment with him. He asked for each person to come into his room individually. From his bed, he embraced each one, offering heartfelt gratitude and personal reflections. He knew these moments would leave a lasting impression, allowing him to connect with each colleague one last time.

Afterward, it was clear to the employees that although they were showing up for Chuck to say their goodbyes, he actually was the one, once again, who showed up for them. His last words to each person modeled such exemplary leadership, making it about them, not himself.

Olivia helped organize the last gathering for Chuck. She said, "You get to choose where you work. You get to choose how you spend your time, your days and your hours, and you always hope that it means something at the end of your life. You hope it was worth it. You're never going to remember the number you hit, or the goals you met, or the quota you did or didn't meet, but you're going to remember the people who mattered to you and the lives you touched and that you mattered to them. I think we were successful with that with Chuck. And he did that for us."

Chuck's story isn't just one of kindness and generosity—it's a blueprint for leadership. He showed that true leadership isn't about authority or titles; it's about connection, trust, and making a difference in the lives of others.

The ripple effects of great leadership extend far beyond

the workplace. When you lead with empathy, purpose, and intentionality, you inspire better performance at work and create a positive impact that touches every area of people's lives. Employees who feel valued and supported by their leader carry that positivity home. They walk through their front doors with less stress, more patience, and a greater sense of fulfillment. They are better partners, parents, and friends because they aren't weighed down by the anxiety of working under poor leadership.

By providing clarity, trust, and encouragement, you help your team avoid the emotional toll of uncertainty and micromanagement. This doesn't just enhance productivity—it frees your team to focus on what matters most, both inside and outside of work. Instead of dreading their next workday or reliving workplace frustrations at the dinner table, they can be fully present for their families and friends. They show up at their kids' soccer games with a smile, enjoy conversations over dinner instead of venting about work, and sleep better at night knowing they're part of a supportive team.

You might wonder, *Can I really become this kind of leader?* The answer is yes. Hundreds of leaders who have used the resources, tools, and ideas in this book have transformed their leadership and their lives. Leaders have shared how implementing small but significant changes—like active listening, setting clear priorities, and delegating effectively—created dramatic improvements in their teams. Others have told me how understanding personality styles, giving meaningful feedback, or running better meetings has completely shifted their workplace dynamics. These leaders report not only increased trust and collaboration but also reduced stress, improved morale, and higher performance.

Leadership isn't about being perfect—it's about being intentional. Chuck exemplified that truth, and now you have the tools to do the same.

As you reflect on your own journey, think about how far you've come. When you first stepped into a leadership role, you may have felt overwhelmed, unsure of where to start, or how to earn your team's trust. Leadership might have seemed like more art than science, reserved for natural leaders. But now you know that leadership isn't an art—it's tactical and can be learned.

Throughout this book, you've gained practical tools and strategies to help you earn respect, achieve results, and make a lasting impact. These skills don't just make you a better leader—they make you a better person.

It's now your turn to carry the torch. Start small. Choose one tactic from this book and put it into practice today. Hold a meaningful one-on-one meeting. Take a few moments to listen deeply to someone who needs support. Celebrate a small win with your team. Set aside focused time.

Don't stop there. Share what you've learned. Mentor someone who's just starting their journey. Be the kind of leader who inspires others to become leaders themselves.

Everyone deserves to work for a great leader. Now you have the tools to be one. Go out and build trust. Achieve results. Change lives. And remember: The most important legacy you leave won't be in what you accomplish—it will be in the people whose lives you touch.

The world needs great leaders and is waiting for people like you to rise to the occasion. And now you have the tools to lead with purpose and confidence. You've got this. Go lead.

# ACKNOWLEDGMENTS

**WHEN I FIRST STARTED WORKING ON THIS BOOK,** I wasn't sure what I was getting into. With millions of books in the world, how hard can it be, right? I learned that writing—and birthing—a book takes a village.

Pete Hoelscher helped shape the outline and contributed his expertise to several sections. His sense of humor and competence made it worthwhile to get up for our early morning meetings.

Thank you to Dr. Gena Cox for graciously sharing her time and author experience and introducing me to Anjanette (AJ) Harper's Top 3 Workshop and Dorie Clark's Recognized Expert training. Little did I know that the communities that these two individuals built would be worth far more than the cost of their programs.

If you want to write a must-read book, AJ Harper's guidance is second to none. Thank you for patiently working with me when early on I was convinced that readers prefer bullet points and flowcharts over stories. AJ warned us about the trolls—the voices in our heads that would whisper doubts, question our work, and tempt us to quit. I didn't believe that, viewing myself egotistically as someone who gets things done.

She was right, of course, and the trolls showed up multiple times. It was the Top 3 Author Community who provided the support needed to keep going. Thank you to all the Top 3 authors who cheered me on and reminded me that what I was writing mattered.

A big thank you to Laura Stone, AJ's Dean of Students and organizational ninja with the heart and soul of a cheerleader. Her encouragement and behind-the-scenes magic made this process smoother than it had any right to be.

Dorie Clark's Recognized Expert (RExer) program is a gem for entrepreneurs. The RExer community answered questions, voted on book titles and cover designs, and provided support on several topics.

The Trilogy Alumni community also responded to polls, provided useful feedback on multiple book titles and book covers, and participated in interviews.

Thank you to Mark Grosvenor, a supportive executive who genuinely cares about developing his team and leading by example. Much of the Practical Leadership Framework and content was developed and tested based on work sponsored by him.

Many others generously shared their time with me for interviews, feedback on early chapters, and/or served as early readers. Thank you to Nicole Anderson, Margaret Andrews, Raymond Beaumont, Margo Boster, Tom Carter, Emmanuel Chavane, Ariane Cline, Chris Copeland, Teri Cote, Lori Durham, Janet Eden-Harris, Sarah Fisher, Keri Glitch, Debra Sabatini Hennelly, Ron Hinsley, Kyle Hosford, Bill Huffaker, Pradeep Ittycheria, Emily Kahren, Cal Kellogg, Greg Kipfmiller, Jazlyn Kraft, Jacob Leffler, Jenny Lisk, Janine Mathó, Angie Mendenhall, Jen Minelli, Dawn Moldenhour, Frank Natividad,

Trey Nelson, Kaylin Orr, Paul Peterson, Lisa Petoskey, Pam Rains, Katie Russell, Peter Scheytt, Sumeet Shendrikar, Catherine Sherwood, Cody Shilts, Marty Sunde, Vennesa Van Ameyde, Michelle Weatherson, Tim Welch, Greg Wempe, Pat Wooley, and Sherri Wooten.

Thank you to Maren Showkeir and Kristina Paider, who better organized the content and shaped the book into a much stronger version.

Brandon Coward brought up thoughtful concerns and asked just the right questions—the kind that helped make this book's content sharper and more authentic. Thank you for your patience and editorial brilliance, going above and beyond.

My partner, Tammi Terry, has been with me every step of the way. Thank you for always helping when I asked, "Can I run something by you?" or "Would you read this, please?" I appreciate you taking care of everything, encouraging me along the way, and giving me the space to write.

# NOTES

**Introduction: Let's Get Practical**

1  Karissa McKenna and Samir Mehta, "The 4 Essential Leadership Roles of Every Career Journey," Center for Creative Leadership, February 15, 2024, https://www.ccl.org/articles/leading-effectively-articles/4-leadership-roles-successful-professional-must-play.

2  Stephanie Neal and Rosey Rhyne, *Leadership Transitions Report 2021*, Developmental Dimensions International Inc., 2021, https://media.ddiworld.com/research/glf21-leadershiptransitions_final.pdf.

3  Swagatam Basu, Atrijit Das, Vitorio Bretas, and Jonah Shepp, "4 Reasons Why Managers Fail," *Harvard Business Review*, April 11, 2024, https://hbr.org/2024/04/4-reasons-why-managers-fail.

**Part 1: Lead by Example**

1  Leslie A. Perlow and Jessica L. Porter, "Making Time Off Predictable—and Required," *Harvard Business Review*, October 2009, https://hbr.org/2009/10/making-time-off-predictable-and-required.

2  Simon Sinek, X, January 28, 2015, https://x.com/simonsinek/status/560513329148723202?lang=en.

3  Dominic Catacora, "Deloitte Finds Authenticity Crisis: 60% 'Identity Covering' at Work Despite DEI Efforts," Future of Work/AllWork, June 7, 2024, https://allwork.space/2024/06/deloitte-finds-authenticity-crisis-60-identity-covering-at-work-despite-dei-efforts/.

4  Evan W. Carr, Andrew Reece, Gabriella Rosen Kellerman, and Alexi Robichaux, "The Value of Belonging at Work," *Harvard Business Review*, December 16, 2019, https://hbr.org/2019/12/

the-value-of-belonging-at-work.

5 Amy C. Edmondson, "Leading in Tough Times: HBS Faculty Member Amy C. Edmondson on Psychological Safety," Harvard Business School Q&A, November 22, 2022, https://www.hbs.edu/recruiting/insights-and-advice/blog/post/leading-in-tough-times.

6 "Understand Team Effectiveness," Google, https://rework.withgoogle.com/en/guides/understanding-team-effectiveness.

7 Amy Edmondson, "Psychological Safety Does Not Equal 'Anything Goes,'" AmyCEdmondson.com, https://amycedmondson.com/psychological-safety-%E2%89%A0-anything-goes/.

8 Kim Scott, *Radical Candor: How to Get What You Want By Saying What You Mean* (St. Martin's Press, 2019).

9 Clayton M. Christensen, "How Will You Measure Your Life? Don't Reserve Your Best Business Thinking for Your Career," *Harvard Business Review*, July-August 2010, https://hbr.org/2010/07/how-will-you-measure-your-life.

**Part 2: Awareness**

1 Lawrence Hamilton, *Conspiracy vs. Science: A Survey of U.S. Public Beliefs*, University of New Hampshire, Carsey School of Public Policy, April 25, 2022, https://carsey.unh.edu/publication/conspiracy-vs-science-survey-us-public-beliefs.

2 George Markowsky, "Information Theory—Communication, Coding, Cryptography," Britannica, last updated June 6, 2025, https://www.britannica.com/science/information-theory/Classical-information-theory.

3 David Rock, *Your Brain at Work: Strategies for Overcoming Distraction, Regaining Focus, and Working Smarter All Day Long* (HarperCollins, 2009).

4 Stefanie K. Johnson and Jessica F. Kirk, "Dual-anonymization Yields Promising Results for Reducing Gender Bias: A Naturalistic Field Experiment of Applications for *Hubble Space Telescope* Time," *Publications of the Astronomical Society of the Pacific* 132, no. 1009 (2020): 1–6, https://doi.org/10.1088/1538-3873/ab6ce0.

5 Claudia Goldin and Cecilia Rouse, "Orchestrating Impartiality: The Impact of 'Blind' Auditions on Female Musicians," *American*

*Economic Review* 90, no. 4 (2000): 715–741.

6   Marianne Bertrand and Sendhil Mullainathan, "Are Emily and Greg More Employable than Lakisha and Jamal? A Field Experiment on Labor Market Discrimination," *American Economic Review* 90, no. 4 (2004): 991–1013.

7   Patrick Kline, Evan K. Rose, and Christopher R. Walters, "A Discrimination Report Card," Becker Friedman Institute for Economics, The University of Chicago, April 8, 2024, https://bfi.uchicago.edu/insight/research-summary/a-discrimination-report-card/.

8   Alexis Krivkovich, Emily Field, Lareina Yee, Megan McConnell, and Hannah Smith, *Women in the Workplace 2024: The 10th-Anniversary Report*, LeanIn.org and McKinsey & Company, September 17, 2024, https://www.mckinsey.com/featured-insights/diversity-and-inclusion/women-in-the-workplace.

9   SHRM, "New SHRM Research Details Age Discrimination in the Workplace," press release, May 11, 2023, https://www.shrm.org/about/press-room/new-shrm-research-details-age-discrimination-workplace.

10  Travis Bradberry and Jean Greaves, *Emotional Intelligence 2.0* (TalentSmartEQ, 2009).

11  Travis Bradberry, "Why Emotional Intelligence Can Save Your Life?" TalentSmartEQ, June 20, 2022, https://www.talentsmarteq.com/emotional-intelligence-can-boost-your-career-and-save-your-life.

12  Daniel Goleman, *Working with Emotional Intelligence* (Bantam Dell, 1998).

13  Viktor E. Frankl, *Man's Search for Meaning* (Beacon Press, 1959).

**Part 3: Effective Communication**

1   Stephen R. Covey, *The 7 Habits of Highly Effective People* (Simon & Schuster, 1989).

2   Ann Latham, *The Power of Clarity: Unleash the True Potential of Workplace Productivity, Confidence, and Empowerment* (Bloomsbury Business, 2021).

3   Lou Solomon, "Two-Thirds of Managers Are Uncomfortable Communicating with Employees," *Harvard Business Review*, March 9, 2016, https://hbr.org/2016/03/

two-thirds-of-managers-are-uncomfortable-communicat-ing-with-employees.

4    VitalSmarts, "Costly Conversations: Why the Way Employees Communicate Will Make or Break Your Bottom-Line," PR Newswire, December 6, 2016, https://www.prnewswire.com/news-releases/costly-conversations-why-the-way-employees-communicate-will-make-or-break-your-bottom-line-300373350.html.

5    Jordan Christiansen, "Costly Conversations: How Lack of Communication is Costing Organizations Thousands in Revenue," Crucial Learning, February 3, 2022, https://cruciallearning.com/press/costly-conversations-how-lack-of-communication-is-costing-organiza-tions-thousands-in-revenue.

6    Douglas Stone, Bruce Patton, and Sheila Heen, *Difficult Conversations: How to Discuss What Matters Most* (Penguin Books, 1999).

## Part 4: Productivity Habits

1    Alex Kerai, "Cell Phone Usage Statistics 2023: Mornings Are for Notifications," Reviews.org, May 9, 2023, https://www.reviews.org/mobile/2023-cell-phone-addiction.

2    Kermit Pattison, "Worker, Interrupted: The Cost of Task Switching," *Fast Company*, July 28, 2008, https://www.fastcompany.com/944128/worker-interrupted-cost-task-switching.

3    David Rock, *Your Brain at Work: Strategies for Overcoming Distraction, Regaining Focus, and Working Smarter All Day Long (HarperCollins, 2009).*

4    Benjamin Spall and Michael Xander, *My Morning Routine: How Successful People Start Every Day Inspired* (Portfolio, 2018).

5    Robin Sharma, *The 5 AM Club: Own Your Morning, Elevate Your Life* (HarperCollins, 2018).

6    Niki Britton, "NTSB: Snapchat Post Caused Fatal Distraction," AOPA, September 13, 2023, https://www.aopa.org/news-and-media/all-news/2023/september/13/ntsb-reports-snapchat-post-caused-fatal-distraction.

7    Harold Pashler, "Task Switching and Multitask Performance," UCSD, July 26, 2002, https://laplab.ucsd.edu/articles/

Pashler_taskswitching_2000.pdf.

8   Joshua S. Rubinstein, David E. Meyer, and Jeffrey E. Evans, "Executive Control of Cognitive Processes in Task Switching," *Journal of Experimental Psychology: Human Perception and Performance* 27, no. 4 (2001): 763–97, https://doi.org/10.1037/0096-1523.27.4.763.

9   Ram Charan, Steve Drotter, and Jim Noel, *The Leadership Pipeline: How to Build the Leadership-Powered Company* (Jossey-Bass, 2011).

10  James Clear, *Atomic Habits: An Easy & Proven Way to Build Good Habits & Break Bad Ones* (Avery, 2018).

11  Dan Sullivan and Dr. Benjamin Hardy, *10X Is Easier Than 2X: How World-Class Entrepreneurs Achieve More by Doing Less* (Hay House, 2023).


**Part 5: Exceptional Results**

1   Michael Bloch, Sven Blumberg, and Jürgen Laartz, "Delivering Large-Scale IT Projects on Time, on Budget, and on Value," McKinsey, October 1, 2012, https://www.mckinsey.com/capabilities/mckinsey-digital/our-insights/delivering-large-scale-it-projects-on-time-on-budget-and-on-value.

2   "The State of Business Communication," Grammarly, 2022, https://www.grammarly.com/business/Grammarly_The_State_Of_Business_Communication.pdf.

3   Detailed information and tactics about how to lead large, complex programs are covered in my book *Luck Is Not a Strategy: An Executive Guidebook for Leading Change Initiatives* (Pendere Press, 2021).


**Part 6: High-Performing Teams**

1   Steve Gruenert and Todd Whitaker, *School Culture Rewired: Toward a More Positive and Productive School for All* (ASCD, 2024).

2   Patrick Guggenberger, Dana Maor, Michael Park, and Patrick Simon, *The State of Organizations 2023: Ten Shifts Transforming Organizations*, McKinsey, April 26, 2023, https://www.mckinsey.com/capabilities/people-and-organizational-performance/our-insights/the-state-of-organizations-2023.

3   Dr. Sabrina Starling, *How to Hire the Best: The Entrepreneur's*

*Ultimate Guide to Attracting Top Performing Team Members* (SKK Enterprises, Inc., 2020).

4 "Why the Onboarding Experience Is Key for Retention," Gallup, https://www.gallup.com/workplace/235121/why-onboarding-experience-key-retention.aspx.

5 Arlene S. Hirsch, "Don't Underestimate the Importance of Good Onboarding," SHRM, August 10, 2017, https://www.shrm.org/topics-tools/news/talent-acquisition/dont-underestimate-importance-good-onboarding.

6 Ron Carucci, "To Retain New Hires, Spend More Time Onboarding Them," *Harvard Business Review*, December 3, 2018, https://hbr.org/2018/12/to-retain-new-hires-spend-more-time-onboarding-them.

7 Gartner, "Gartner HR Research Finds Only 31% of Employees Report They Are Engaged, Enthusiastic and Energized by Their Work," press release, October 24, 2023, https://www.gartner.com/en/newsroom/press-releases/2023-10-24-rhr-gartner-hr-research-finds-only-31-percent-of-employees-report-they-are-engaged.

8 *State of the Global Workplace 2025 Report*, Gallup, https://www.gallup.com/workplace/349484/state-of-the-global-workplace.aspx.

# ABOUT THE AUTHOR

**JANET PLY, PHD,** is a leadership consultant with more than twenty-five years of experience working with companies ranging from start-ups to Fortune 50.

In her work with organizations such as Northrop Grumman, Tyson Foods, Fidelity Systems Company, and AT&T Solutions, she has served as an adviser to dozens of C-suite executives, spearheaded recovery of large ($600 million-plus) initiatives, led strategic planning sessions, streamlined and automated business processes, developed program management offices, and facilitated hands-on leadership and project management workshops.

Rather than approaching leadership development from organizational development or human resources perspectives, she approaches it from life in the trenches, where she experienced leadership (or lack thereof) and the consequences firsthand.

She holds a bachelor's degree in mathematics, master's degrees in engineering and procurement and acquisition, and a PhD in information technology and is certified through the John Maxwell Group as a DiSC consultant, speaker, trainer, and coach.

She is also the author of *Luck Is Not a Strategy: An Executive Guidebook for Leading Change Initiatives*, which provides tactics for positioning large-scale initiatives to be successful from the start and how to get them to the finish line.